HITTING THE CURVEBALLS

"The basic fundamentals that carry one to success against all odds in business are also the fundamentals that carry one to success in family, faith, and all other aspects of life. Jay Myers's journey illustrates this fact, and his candid, honest account of his personal path in *Hitting the Curveballs* is an illuminating look into how courage, character, and perseverance steadied him through the most trying times. What makes *Hitting the Curveballs* special isn't that it's so dissimilar from countless others; rather it is the heartfelt candor with which Jay allows us into his personal path, thoughts, and feelings that compels and inspires others to maintain their own path that makes this a great read."

—**Bill Courtney**, Star of the 2012
Academy Award–winning documentary ***Undefeated***

"Bouncing back from adversity is a real test of character and courage. Clearly Jay Myers has overcome many business and personal challenges and yet maintains such a positive outlook. That is so inspiring for others who face similar challenges. I appreciate his honesty and willingness to share this with others. I highly recommend *Hitting the Curveballs* for every small business owner. Go Yankees!"

—**Chuck Wilson**, Executive Director, NSCA

"During the four-year period (2007–11) that included the great recession, ISI grew from $11 million to $25 million. Jay shares with us the secrets he and his team used to realize this phenomenal growth. In *Hitting the Curveballs*, Jay shares with us proven and tested practical ideas for growing your business in today's challenging economic environment."

—**Madan Birla**, Author of ***FedEx Delivers***

"There is a word in Finnish that is used with pride: SISU. With SISU Finns have managed to build their reputation, be it in music (Jean Sibelius), architecture (Elial Saarinen), sports (Teemu Selanne), or world politics (President Ahtisaari). Jay Myers tells his own SISU story in *Hitting the Curveballs*: personal, honest, and full of energy."

—**Matti Copeland**, Chief Curiosity Officer
Founder of www.mcreads.com

"Seeing an entrepreneur enjoying success is like observing an Olympic athlete on the podium with a gold medal. In that moment of admiration, what you don't see is the years of work, great risk endured, adversity overcome, and doubts slayed. In his new book *Hitting the Curveballs*, Jay Myers pulls back the curtain to reveal components of the "all in" commitment required for entrepreneurial greatness. This is a gift—take it. Thanks, Jay."

—**Jim Blasingame**, small business expert,
author, and syndicated columnist
Host of *The Small Business Advocate* show

"Jay Myers embraces and inspires today's leaders to not just accept trouble as it comes, but to grow through trouble."

—**Dr. Phil Bryant**, Assistant Professor of Management
Columbus State University

HITTING THE CURVE BALLS

How Crisis Can Strengthen and Grow Your Business

JAY MYERS

New York

HITTING THE CURVEBALLS

How Crisis Can Strengthen and Grow Your Business

ISBN 978-1-61448-716-6 paperback
ISBN 978-1-61448-717-3 eBook
Library of Congress Control Number: 2013938798

Morgan James Publishing
The Entrepreneurial Publisher
5 Penn Plaza, 23rd Floor
New York City, New York 10001
(212) 655-5470 office • (516) 908-4496 fax
www.MorganJamesPublishing.com

Cover Design by:
Rachel Lopez
www.r2cdesign.com

Interior Design by:
Bonnie Bushman
bonnie@caboodlegraphics.com

In an effort to support local communities, raise awareness and funds, Morgan James Publishing donates a percentage of all book sales for the life of each book to Habitat for Humanity Peninsula and Greater Williamsburg.

Get involved today, visit
www.MorganJamesBuilds.com.

To my wife, Maureen, whose courage and resilience have been a source of inspiration to me each and every day. I am a better person for having married you thirty years later.

And to my son, Jordan, and daughter, Kaitlin, who continue to make me proud in everything you do. Being your father is the greatest job in the world.

CONTENTS

INTRODUCTION

FIELD OF DREAMS

Yankee Stadium
August 4, 2008

I'm standing in front of Yankee Stadium, and I'm nervous—real nervous. What time did they tell us to be here? Was it seven a.m. or seven thirty? How should I know? I didn't sleep a wink last night. Getting a chance to play baseball in the same place where the New York Yankees have won twenty-six world championships? Are you kidding me?

Okay, I admit it: I am a really crazy baseball fan. My favorite team has always been the New York Yankees even though I grew up in Memphis. How did that happen? You see my dad was a huge Mickey Mantle fan (both of them grew up in Oklahoma) If Mickey wasn't God in my house, he was at least his little brother. But truth be known, I really just love the game—period.

I remember playing Little League baseball as a kid. I'd be so excited to play that the day before every game, I would carefully lay out my uniform on my bed, and then check and double-check the weather forecast to make sure it wasn't calling for rain.

And now I'm at the New York Yankees Fantasy Camp with thirty other crazy baseball fans, here to live the dream of playing in the same stadium as Yankee legends Reggie Jackson, Mickey Mantle, Joe DiMaggio, Babe Ruth, and Lou Gehrig.

Another fantasy camper named Karl walks up. "You here to play ball?" he asks with a grin.

"Sure am," I reply.

"Sleep much last night?" he asks.

"Not a wink," I reply.

"Me either," Karl says. I'm glad I'm not the only one who is so jacked up to play ball in such a famous place.

A few minutes later, Karl and I are joined by a number of other campers excited about the once-in-a-lifetime opportunity. We walk slowly into the stadium and head for the locker room. "You see that picture, Karl?" I ask.

"You mean the one with Lou Gehrig?" he replies.

"Yeah. You don't see that everywhere."

As we proceed further through the famous stadium, we see other pictures: Mickey Mantle, Billy Martin, Bobby Murcer, and of course, Babe Ruth. It's like walking through a history book.

As Karl and I continue the conversation, I find out that he is an attorney in New York City for Bloomberg LP, the mayor's media company. He has a big-time job with a bunch of attorneys reporting to him. But on this Monday morning in August 2008, he's just like the rest of us, pretending to be a kid for a day and excited about playing the game we all love so much in our favorite stadium.

Known as the Cathedral of Baseball, Yankee Stadium was constructed in the Bronx for $2.4 million dollars (equal to $32,737,500 today) between 1922 and 1923. It was built specifically for the Yankees, who had been sharing the Polo Grounds with the New York Giants baseball team for ten years. Yankee Stadium opened during the 1923 Major League Baseball season, and at the time it was hailed as a one-of-a-kind facility in our country for its size. Over the course of its history, it became one of the most famous venues in the United States, having hosted a variety of events and historic moments during its existence. While many of these moments were baseball-related—including World Series games, no-hitters, perfect games, and historic home runs—the stadium also hosted boxing matches, concerts, conventions of Jehovah's Witnesses, and three papal masses. The stadium went through many alterations and playing surface configurations over the years. The condition of the facility worsened in the 1960s and 1970s, prompting its closing for renovation from 1974 to 1975. The renovation significantly altered the appearance of the venue and reduced the distance of the outfield fences. The stadium hosted 6,581 regular season Yankee home games during its eighty-five-year history, and hosted thirty-seven World Series from 1923 to 2003.

And on this August morning in 2008, a bunch of crazy fans are dressed up in Yankee uniforms and playing a game in this historic site. We all ask ourselves, *What could be better?*

We dress in the famous pinstripe uniforms and head through the corridor leading up to the dugout, and that's when I see it. I do a double-take. It's the famous sign with the quote from Joe DiMaggio, and I get goose bumps. Then I pinch myself to make sure it's really happening and read it again: "I want to thank the good Lord for making me a Yankee." I'm so excited I'm shaking, and we're not even on the field yet.

And then we trot out onto the famous turf and take a deep breath. Unreal. I ask myself, *What am I doing here?* I stopped playing competitive baseball when I was in seventh grade, way back in 1969. Richard Nixon was president. In other words, a very long time ago. It's crazy, but hey, I'm here. As I look at my teammates, I see a variety of sizes and ages. Some guys played college baseball—and from all appearances, not too long ago. I'm trying to hide my anxiety, but I'm not doing a very good job. Then I look around and realize everyone is anxious. One guy is chewing his gum so fast that I think he's going to either swallow his tongue or break a few teeth. Or both.

A couple of minutes later, out of the dugout come the Yankee legends: Goose Gossage, Ron Guidry, Bucky Dent, Tim Raines, Jeff Nelson, Oscar Gamble, Jesse Barfield, and others. In their era, the best in the game. And we're playing baseball against these guys? Seriously?

At that point, it hits us. This is going to happen. We are really going to play baseball in the most famous ballpark in the world against the New York Yankees. Older or not, these guys were real players, and I'm thinking, *Once a player, always a player.*

We stand at home plate. The same place where Josh Hamilton hit thirty five home runs in the Home Run Derby at the All-Star Game just a few days ago. The same home plate where Reggie Jackson hit three home runs in a game in the 1977 World Series. And the same home plate where Mickey Mantle, Joe DiMaggio, Babe Ruth, and Lou Gehrig hit all those home runs all those years ago.

Did I just hear that the regular Yankee announcer, Michael Kay, is doing the play-by-play? I'm not sure if it's a rumor, but someone said the game was going to be shown on the YES Network. That would be the Yankees Entertainment and Sports Network. For us? Must be somebody's idea of a joke.

Is Al Downing really doing the color commentary? The same Al Downing who used to pitch for the Yankees and gave up the famous record-setting home run to Hank Aaron? It was surreal.

In an effort to burn off the excess energy, we start running around the stadium. We run to right field and pause for a moment. Wow, this is the position that the immortal Babe Ruth once played all those years ago. The greatest baseball player of all time, and we're standing where he once stood. It's too crazy, so we keep running. We run to center field and do the same thing. Joe DiMaggio and Mickey Mantle played right where we're standing. This is sacred ground, and we all know it. Didn't every Little League ballplayer in the country dream of one day playing center field for the Yankees? We go through the same ritual in left field and then get ready for batting practice.

No pressure there—except when you have Yankee legends like Mickey Rivers, Bucky Dent, Goose Gossage, and Jesse Barfield

Field of Dreams. *One of the more intimidating experiences of my life was having Mickey Rivers, Bucky Dent, Goose Gossage, and Jesse Barfield watching me in batting practice.*

Pre-Game Batting Practice. *Getting some useful
tips from former home run champ Jesse Barfield.*

watching you. And how about getting a batting tip from a guy who hit
241 home runs in the majors with the Blue Jays and Yankees and won
the 1986 home run title? I'm standing in, taking a few good whacks at
the ball, when Jesse pulls me aside. He points out a certain way I need
to follow through to get better contact on the ball.

What happened next will be a memory I will have for the rest of
my life. Yankee coach Tony Ferrara throws one right over the plate,
and I hit the ball harder than I ever have in my whole life. It goes to
deep center—in Yankee Stadium. I get out of the batting cage and
Jesse gives me a big bear hug. "That's what I'm talking about," he says.
I'm pumped. Even Goose and Bucky are grinning. I cannot believe
what I just did. I've waited more than fifty years to get to this point,
ever since I was kid I dreamed of putting on the Yankee uniform and
playing ball in this stadium. It's been a long road to get here for me,
but I am truly living the dream.

As we line up for the national anthem, I must say I get a little
choked up, a little overwhelmed. And then, when the two words "Play
ball" are uttered, the fantasy really begins.

From that point on, it's like everything is in slow motion. When it's finally my turn to bat, I'm so nervous I can barely stand up. And why not? I'm facing Jeff Nelson, all 6'8" of him. Jeff Nelson, who played for four World Series Championship teams with the Yankees in 1996–2000. Hell, he even played in the 2003 World Series. That was a short five years ago. I'm thinking, *Are you kidding me?* When we were all warming up, I did make a request: "Don't hurt me, okay?" Sure hope he remembers.

Hitting the Curveball. *Battling Jeff Nelson in Yankee Stadium that August morning in 2008 was a once-in-a-lifetime experience.*

The rest is a little blurry. "Strike one," the umpire barks. I back off the plate. I don't remember seeing the ball. *Hey, Jeff, this is for fun,* I'm thinking. Then I remember he has struck out our first six batters at that point. What did our best player say? "Fantasy? This is a freaking nightmare." He then proceeded to bash his bat into the water cooler. *This should be fun,* I'm thinking.

The next pitch, Jeff decides to really hum it right in there but misses the plate. I breathe a sigh of relief. Ball one. Thank God. Then

Fantasy Camp 2008. *Pretty cool to have your own cheering section in Yankee Stadium: Maureen Myers (left) and her sister Beth (right).*

he throws another one in close, and I take the bait. "Strike two"—and I'm not feeling so good. I dig in a little deeper. And then he throws The Pitch. The one I was waiting for. I can tell as soon as I hear the loud crack that I did good. The ball seems to jump off my bat, and I am so excited. I hear the cheers from the crowd (okay, my wife and her sister), as it looks like my ball is dropping in for a hit.

A Great Hit. *Even if it was just batting practice, hitting it to deep center in Yankee Stadium was special.*

I race to first base, only to see the Yankee second baseman, Pat Kelly, make a circus catch and pull it in. "Damn," I blurt out and trot back to the dugout, disappointed. It sure would have been nice. "Sorry guys, I thought it was a hit," I tell my teammates. But in reality, if truth be known, I'm just glad to be here. And after last summer, who wouldn't be?

Then it hit me. Was it just a year ago? God, it seems like it's been much longer than that. I'm here at Yankee Stadium, living the dream, and I wouldn't be here if it weren't for my company's success. But it has not come easy, for me or Interactive Solutions (ISI). Talk about getting hit with some curveballs.

Starting with that tumultuous summer of 2007, my business and my life got hit with the biggest curveballs you could imagine. Key team members left without warning. One employee passed away unexpectedly. My wife was diagnosed with cancer. And there was that tiny detail of the Great Recession.

But despite these challenges, somehow we also experienced the greatest rate of growth in our company's history, going from $11 million to more than $25 million in revenue in four years.

As I said, I'm a crazy baseball fan. Maybe it's because it's the only sport I was pretty good at as a kid, or maybe it's more than that. Baseball is all about statistics and history. Baseball fans like me still like to talk about who won the 1956 Triple Crown (Mickey Mantle) and who won the 1960 World Series (the Pittsburgh Pirates). Or maybe in the crazy, fast-paced world that we live in, it's just the simple pace of the game. It's so methodical and calculated. You really can't speed up a baseball game. It's going to take three hours or so to play a nine-inning game, no matter what happens. Maybe that's why I love it so much. No hurry-up. Slow and steady. And it is America's pastime. Time to unwind and relax at a measured pace.

So it's probably not a surprise that I took the same approach that I love so much about baseball with my business. No hurry-up. Slow and steady. Take it at a measured pace. View the unexpected as positive opportunities rather than negative threats. These were the principles behind our success during a time when many strong businesses went under.

Growing a business in any economy is a tough task, but in a recession it's even more difficult—and definitely not for the faint of heart. Money is tight, competition is keen, and customers are more demanding than ever before. For a number of businesses, it has simply been too much to handle: more than 200,000 small businesses in the United States closed down between 2008 and 2010.

With the closing of their doors, these same businesses have also taken with them more than three million jobs, according to census figures, and represent the greatest economic downturn in the United States since the Great Depression more than 80 years ago. Those statistics are both scary and depressing.

Given all the uncertainty and challenges in the nation's economy, how can a small business survive these difficult times? Is it just way too risky? Is it time to throw in the towel? Would anybody really blame a small business owner if that's what he or she chose to do?

In this book, I'd like to share the principles that helped my company, ISI, hit the curveballs and turn crisis into an opportunity for growth beyond anything I had expected. I believe any company can apply these principles when crisis hits and bring out the best in its business when everyone else is panicking. In fact, these principles are not just for recessions or crises, but should be part of your company's habits, no matter what the economy or your competition is doing.

I admit, I'm a storyteller by nature. So, although I hope this book will share some practical advice for entrepreneurs and business owners, the best way I know how to share that practical advice is by telling the stories of how I learned these principles myself. When you hear the stories, I hope you'll find it will be even easier to figure out how you can apply them to your business. And at the end of each chapter, you'll find a section called "Stepping Up to the Plate" that summarizes how these same principles can be used to effectively grow your business.

So let's go back to that summer before Yankee Stadium . . . the summer when all hell broke loose.

CHAPTER 1

THE SUMMER FROM HELL

In my book *Keep Swinging*, I wrote about the day my business almost died, when we discovered our trusted employee had stolen more than $257,000 from my company. Yet we survived. In fact, my company, ISI, even doubled business to $10 million the year after the embezzlement. Not that there wasn't a cost. When someone violates your trust, it takes a long time to get it back.

Even so, emerging from that experience left me with a feeling of incredible gratitude. I was grateful for my wife, grateful for my children, and grateful to live in a country that allows goofballs like me to build a business out of dirt. Since 1996, ISI had grown like a weed, from $262,000 in sales to a little more than $11 million, despite the many market challenges in the technology industry as well as the poor rural territory that the company covers. By the summer of 2007, we thought we had seen it all.

June 26, 2007

I was at my desk when I got the call. It was from my vice president of design and engineering, Derek Plummer, my right-hand man and most trusted employee. "Did you check your voice mail?" Derek asked.

"Not yet," I replied.

"You might want to do that," Derek suggested.

"Is everything okay?" I asked.

"Just check your voice mail," he said.

When I accessed my voice mail, it was a message from ISI's CTO (Chief Technology Officer) and leading salesman. " Resigning from the company" is all I really heard even though he also mentioned something about starting his own company.

I slammed down the phone. *Are you kidding me? The guy has been with me more than nine years, and this is how he leaves me? By leaving a voice mail message?* I could barely talk, I was so mad. What the hell just happened? This guy had been making good money for a number of years. Really good money. What was the issue? And what went wrong?

Yes, our CTO was also ISI's leading salesman (he had that kind of talent). He produced 50 percent of our revenue and was part of the original success of the company in the late 1990s. He had sold more than $20 million since he started with me in 1998 and had really helped grow the company. And I never missed the chance to tell him how much I appreciated the work he had done for us. When I thought of him, I thought of the old days. All of us bootstrapping our way to success. All about teamwork.

We had accomplished a lot since we started in 1996, making the *Inc.* magazine list of fastest-growing private companies in the United States twice, in 2001 and 2003, and earning numerous other awards that we should be proud of. How about the fact that only 4 percent of start-ups make it to the tenth year?[1] Shouldn't everyone at ISI feel grateful for all the success we were continuing to have? Didn't our CTO know what a good deal he had? Apparently not everyone shared that sentiment. Our CTO was the second to leave that eventful summer, following the vice president of customer service three weeks earlier.

Losing support personnel was one thing, but losing a guy who produced more than $4 million in revenue every year was a horse of a different color. This was definitely going to be a challenge. And then the mind games started. *What was going on? And what was next? Would there be more to come?* As I pondered those thoughts, I was also trying to stay positive. It definitely hurt me both personally and professionally to lose a tenured employee, but I had to soldier on. Then again, I didn't really have a choice, did I? I went home that night, thinking that maybe this was just a big misunderstanding and I'd wake up the next day and we'd work it all out.

After tossing and turning all night long and getting absolutely no sleep, the next morning I called our CTO to question him. "What's the deal?" I asked. "Are you really resigning after all these years?"

He said very little and then finally muttered an apology. "I guess I should have treated you better," he said. "We have been together a long time and I've always had a lot of respect for you."

"You have a helluva way of showing it," I respond. And thus a wonderful nine-and-a-half-year relationship ended with one phone call.

July 4, 2007

Outside of the chaos at the office, at home it seemed like a regular old summer, until we got a call from a good friend on vacation with

---

1   Michael E. Gerber, *The E Myth: Why Most Small Businesses Don't Work and What to Do About It* (Harper Business, 1990).

her family down in Gulf Shores, Alabama. Her husband, Mike, had gotten really sick with some flulike symptoms while they were on the beach one day and had gotten steadily worse—so much so that she had to drive him to a larger hospital in Meridian, Mississippi. Some doctors there were better equipped to treat him, she was told. It was all happening too fast to comprehend, but it looked like he wasn't going to make it.

Mike and I had been close for a number of years. He was a good friend and fellow baseball fanatic. In fact, just a few months ago we had played golf with Tom Tresh, the former Yankee who had played ball with Mickey Mantle in the 1960s. The event was the 2006 Redbirds Classic, hosted by the Memphis Redbirds AAA baseball team, which was held each year to benefit the Reviving Baseball in Inner Cities (RBI) program in Memphis. RBI donates bats, balls, and gloves to needy children interested in playing baseball. It was a worthy cause, and we had such a great time that day, meeting old baseball legends like Ken Griffey, Tommy John, and Manny Sanguillén. Neither of us wanted to go home. (That's the sign of a true baseball fan. You love the game so much you soak up every second you can just to be around it.)

And it wasn't just baseball. Our wives and our kids have been friends for years. In fact, all four kids had been on the country club swim team together since they were little. Wasn't it just yesterday we were all hanging around the pool cheering for the kids, rooting them on, watching them win all those ribbons and trophies, celebrating with cookouts at our house? We had been close for so many years. Mike was in his early fifties and in good shape—at least, I thought he was. Yet my friend was dying.

Several hours later we got the call that confirmed our worst fears. Mike had died. Just a few days ago, he was enjoying his vacation on the beautiful white sandy beaches of Gulf Shores, Alabama, and then he was gone. My family and I were all too stunned to know what to do next. Ironically enough, Mike died on Independence Day. The all-American guy, baseball fan, ex-Marine, and patriot died on our country's birthday. He was a good man who left us way too early.

As my family and I tried to wrap ourselves around our emotions and shared grief, we didn't know another jolt was coming. This one was closer to home.

July 14, 2007

10 days later, I was in my closet changing my shirt so I could go to Mike's memorial service when the phone rang, and I answered the call from one of my managers. "Doesn't look like Danney's going to make it," he said.

"Oh my God," I replied. "How long does he have?"

"Maybe not but a few days or so," came the reply.

I'm trying to compose myself but having a hard time of it. How can this be happening?

I knew Danney was in for a tough haul when he had first gotten sick. It was some kind of liver problem, and he was going to need to be off work for quite a while. We'd been told he would need some serious surgery and likely a transplant. Several ISI employees had already donated blood to help him out. They knew how serious it was. We had never faced life-and-death issues with an employee of ISI before, and it was scary. A transplant? Tough news, and I was concerned. Danney was my employee, but he was also a part of the ISI family. And we take that very seriously. We are all in it together, whatever it is—good, bad, or otherwise.

Danney was also one of the best technicians we had and had built a helluva reputation for not only his hard work but also his ability to do some amazing things installing our technology. Danney was also one of my favorite employees for a lot of reasons, but mainly because he was so low maintenance, just an old-fashioned worker bee. In all the years he worked for me, I never once heard him whine or complain. He just put his head down and got 'er done. He was a good guy with a great work ethic.

I wished I had twenty installers like him. And now Danney was in trouble. Big trouble. I felt helpless. I may have been just the business owner, but I wanted to do something more for him. I felt responsible for him. I wanted to fix this. That's what I do at ISI. I fix stuff. But as I would discover, this was something way beyond what I could fix.

In the days that followed, I kept telling our staff that it's very simple with me and ISI: When one hurts, we all hurt. And we were all concerned about Danney.

It was hard to concentrate on anything after that. Work doesn't seem to matter when you have an employee in such a tough situation.

One of our guys did some research. I was told that Danney should have a good chance for survival. In fact, in 2007, 6,493 liver transplants were performed worldwide, while 16,761 patients continued to be on the waiting list for transplantation. Chances of survival following orthotopic liver transplantation are generally good, with a five-year survival rate of 72 percent. The most common causes of death in liver transplant patients (beyond the early in-hospital transplant period) are infection, rejection, and malignancy. His chances looked pretty good, or at least we thought so.

However, after his transplant operation, the doctors were concerned about rejection. Danney struggled for days and didn't get any better. As more days went by, the situation looked more and more bleak. Then I was told, "Danney is definitely not going to make it. In fact, he is probably not going to live through the night."

My mind was spinning at that point. I thought he was getting better. Liver transplants are done every day, right?

Then we got the call that Danney had passed away. *How could this be? Why Danney? What day is it, anyway? Didn't we just bury Mike, and now we're going to have to bury Danney, too?*

As an entrepreneur, you learn how to do a lot of things to get a business started and to grow it. Sales, service, finance, marketing, recruiting—that's the fun part about being an entrepreneur and starting a business, and it's something I know and understand.

But losing an employee is definitely not in the playbook. I'll never forget the look of grief on my employees' faces at Danney's funeral service. We had all been through so much, and now this. What do I tell them? How can I comfort them? Yes, I'm a control freak. That's one of the reasons that ISI runs a tight ship. I'm in control. But now? I have no idea what to do next.

It really felt like God was piling on at this point. So many bad things happened in such a short period of time that I kept thinking, *Is 2007 another 2003?* To be honest, I was afraid to turn out the lights at night. Why? Because I was scared about what the next day will bring.

It didn't take long to find out.

July 23, 2007

For a month or so my wife Maureen had been going to the doctor to follow up on some mammogram tests that didn't look right. Although we were both concerned, there didn't seem to be any reason for worry, until the latest visit. We learned that the suspicious images on the mammogram were early stage breast cancer. Not the type of news you want to hear. In fact, when we got the news at the doctor's office that day I remember Maureen said my face turned ashen. I wasn't thinking about me; I was thinking about her, and I was worried. Both Maureen and I knew what a breast cancer diagnosis looks like, having experienced it with both her mother, Jean, and my mother, Dorothy, in the late 1980s.

Although science has made a lot of progress in treatment, hearing the word "cancer" can be scary for a lot of reasons. It's scary for the things you know and scary for the things you don't know. Being a melanoma survivor myself, I know a cancer diagnosis can play tricks with your head. You tend to fast-forward to a doomsday scenario even with limited information. This isn't rational thinking; it's fear. Granted, with breast cancer, the statistics are scary. For women in the United States, breast cancer death rates are higher than those for any other cancer besides lung cancer. Besides skin cancer, breast cancer is the most commonly diagnosed cancer among American women. Just under 30 percent of cancers in women are breast cancers. Even though death rates have been decreasing since 1990, especially in women under fifty, 39,520 women in the United States were expected to die in 2007 from breast cancer.

But first things first. What were we dealing with?

What stage was her cancer in? How serious was it? Did we catch it in time, and what were the treatment options? Some doctors wanted to cut it out, others wanted to burn it out, and still others wanted to poison it out. Either way, something had to be done—and done quickly. Breast cancer is like any cancer. Catch it early, and there's a high survival rate. Let it sit around, and it often leads to a whole lot of trouble.

With all this swirling around in our minds, Maureen and I were trying to take it all in and get some questions answered. Her doctors explained that she had a common form of breast cancer called ductal carcinoma in situ, or DCIS, which accounted for approximately 83 percent of in situ cases diagnosed between 2004 and 2007. In fact, there were more than 23,000 in situ cases diagnosed from 1995 to 2007 in the United States alone. It's a disease that had unfortunately become fairly common among women of all ages, but far more prevalent in women over fifty years old. That was the bad news. But the good news was that her cancer was caught early, and it could be treated quickly and with very few potential problems. "Thank God," we both said simultaneously, breathing a collective sigh of relief.

Finally, some good news this summer. But it was also decision time. "What do you want to do?" I asked Maureen.

"I want this behind me as quickly as possible," she said. But there were a couple of choices. She could do the standard radiation treatment, which would take about six weeks, or try a new option that could be done in just one week with two treatments a day. That treatment plan, the MammoSite Radiation Therapy System, was approved by the FDA in May 2002 and was offered as an option because of the type of cancer she had and the fact that her cancer was at a lower stage of development (less than level 1).

MammoSite is a simpler, less invasive method of delivering breast brachytherapy; it's a site-specific radiation treatment completed in four to five days, as compared to six weeks for traditional radiation therapy. Both Maureen and I liked the idea of getting this taken care of as quickly as possible, and five days of treatment sure beat six weeks, but would it really be as effective? Her physician explained that the treatment would deliver radiation directly to the area where the tumor was removed, which is where tumors are most likely to recur, essentially burning out the cancer cells without harming healthy tissue.

The other thing about the MammoSite treatment was that it had to be done close to the time of the original surgical biopsy (which had been done a few days earlier) using the same incision site, before it had time to heal. It might not be a lot of fun, but it would all be done in a short amount of time. Maureen's treatment would be Monday through Friday for one week, and then follow-up visits every few months for the next few years. "You're a very lucky lady," one doctor said. I'm not sure you can say "lucky" and "cancer" in the same sentence, but it was indeed a blessing, since it could have been far worse.

We decided on the date for treatment. It was the week of our family vacation in Hilton Head, South Carolina, with our two kids, Jordan and Katie. It was also during the time we had scheduled an interview with Katie's dream college, the Savannah College of Art and Design. If she had to reschedule the interview, she might lose her chance for admission. And Maureen didn't want us to worry about her health. In fact, she kept repeating her doctor's words over and over again: "This is no big deal." The kids and I were concerned but reluctantly decided to go forward with our travel plans. Maureen promised to join us at the end of the week and enjoy a shortened vacation.

What a warrior. Ever since we got married back in 1983, she has always been my inspiration. Unflappable. Always sees the brighter side of things. Always my rock, through thick and thin. She truly embodies grace under fire. Even when I got fired (twice), started the business, dealt with my melanoma diagnosis, went through a partnership divorce, and weathered employee embezzlement. After all the crap I put her through, she still had a smile on her face and was always there to support me.

Now she needed to lean on me. I knew what I needed to do, but I was scared. Scared for her. Scared for me. And scared for my kids. They needed their mother. I needed their mother. But we also needed to see this through.

True to form, choosing not to dwell on the negative side of things, Maureen bravely met the challenge with unbelievable courage. I definitely didn't marry a wimp. Now it was time for me to step up.

July 30, 2007

I think it was about that time that I knew I needed to get away. I certainly didn't plan the family vacation with these events in mind, but it sure came at the right time: we all needed a break.

But when the kids and I left for Hilton Head that day, I must admit I felt more than a little weird. While I understood that Maureen wanted us to keep things as normal as possible, it still didn't seem right to leave her back in Memphis, having to deal with the radiation treatment alone. But she was insistent.

"I want this behind me," she said. "I want you and the kids to go, and I will meet you at Hilton Head this weekend. Take a break and get away."

But how could we enjoy ourselves without her? It didn't seem right, but away we went to get some time to pull ourselves together, pray for Maureen, and reflect on all we had been through the past few weeks. *When was all of this bad stuff going to end? Why was it happening to us? Had we done something wrong?* All these thoughts were going through my head when we arrived at the condo at Hilton Head. It was a Monday morning when I got the next call.

My VP of sales called me on my son's cell phone. I had left my own phone at home because I needed to step away from all the events of the previous few weeks. I had given my son's number to a only few people at the office and told them to call me only if it was a real emergency, like somebody bleeding or dying (or both). So when the call came in, I knew it wasn't good.

"What's going on?" I asked.

"I hate to tell you this, but I'm leaving the company."

"You're kidding," I replied. "What's the deal?"

He explained that he needed a more structured work environment and that it was time to move on. At that point I was shellshocked. *This guy's been with me for more than six years, sold more than $15 million in his career at ISI, and he calls to give me notice while I'm on vacation? Are you serious?* We had not only a strong professional relationship, but a personal one as well. That's the thing about owning a small business—over time, employees feel like family. Which is why I felt so sideswiped. He knew what Maureen and I were going through. After six years, I admit I expected the courtesy of being allowed to finish out my vacation and recoup with my family in peace before having to deal with such a drastic announcement.

The Summer from Hell. *I never thought I would ever see a humorous spin on losing my entire sales team of 2006.*

Leaving ISI was starting to feel like a disease. And it was spreading. I argued with him for a few more minutes about what a mistake he was making before I realized there was no point to it. When I got off the phone, I was devastated. Now the VP of sales was leaving, too, the guy I hired back in 2001, the one guy I thought I could count on. It was a nightmare unfolding in front of my very eyes: my two key sales guys, who represented 80 percent of our sales revenue, were leaving the company within a little more than a month of each other. No warning or advance notice from one, and the other quit while I was on vacation. Wow, some kind of loyalty these guys had. They knew nothing about video conferencing before I hired them and both increased their income dramatically over the last few years, courtesy of good old ISI.

I was having some seriously strong reactions. I thought about why I felt so betrayed. If the tables had been turned and I had struggles with them, I would have given feedback when the problems were small and given them every opportunity to be part of a solution. That's what loyalty is. But they didn't come to me when their problems were small to try to work out a solution; they just abandoned the company when I was at a personal low point and really left me in a bind.

Well, if I was going to have to start over, at least I knew what that was like. Back in 1998, I had start over when I bought out my partner and had to reorganize the company to try to grow it. And in 2003, I certainly had to start over in one sense, when my accounting manager stole $257,000 and almost put ISI out of business.

And there we were in 2007. In just over a month, both an employee and a good friend died, my company's biggest producer and another key employee left the company, and my wife was diagnosed with breast cancer. How much can one person take?

That summer, I was pretty focused on myself. Since I tend to take things so personally, I didn't realize it at the time, but the whole company suffered when these guys left. More than a few ISI employees and managers were downright angry. "You didn't deserve this," they said. "We didn't deserve this. You were good to those guys, and they screwed us."

At the time I agreed with their sentiment, and then some. But the operative word was "us." The turnover on the sales team didn't affect just me; it affected the whole company—and that realization was the first major step forward in dealing with the problem.

The bottom line was that I still had a company to run. What does a leader do in times like this—when we're not riding the victory train?

How do you control the anger and frustration and do something good with it?

I remembered what Michael Bloomberg, the mayor of New York City, said about times like these: "Anger is not a management strategy." I know, it sounds obvious, but in that moment of crisis, it was a lifeline. And it was hard to put into action. I knew one thing: I could do nothing alone. I needed some serious support to get back on track. Where was I going to get that help? Who might provide it?

The answer came to me a short time later, and it was from a totally unexpected source. I would discover that these events weren't just about me. They were going to show us what our company was made of.

CHAPTER 2

BETTING THE FARM

So where did I get this much-needed support? I got it from Derek Plummer, my talented engineering manager who had been with me since 1997 and had seen it all. From the partnership split to the embezzlement crisis and the numerous challenges associated with growing a technology business, Derek has been my constant. He has had my back for years, and I needed him yet again. One thing about Derek: he may not be the most warm and fuzzy guy you'll ever meet, but he is also a guy who doesn't scare easily. I have told him on more than a few occasions that at the end of the day, he is the one guy at ISI who, if need be, I can go into war with. This might not have been a war, but it certainly qualified as a crisis. ISI was hurting, and we needed to get fixed, quickly.

Derek's timing was perfect. He called right after our VP of sales did. "Need some help?" he asked.

"More than you'll ever know," I respond. "Got any ideas?"

"Why don't we get a conference call with the rest of the sales team and give them a pep talk?" Derek suggested. "Maybe give them an idea of what we need from them?"

"We need their support for sure. Let's do it," I replied.

In my heart, I was concerned. How could we pull this off with rookies who had hardly any industry experience?

All three were smart, aggressive young guys, but they were still trying to find their way in the industry. One guy had just started with us, and the other two had experienced some modest success but were still learning. I'm not saying I didn't have faith, but I was nervous and had a good right to be. This may have been just a job to them, but for me it may have been life or death for my company. I had a lot on the line and needed to feel good about all of this. If these guys couldn't get it done, then what? Did I need to hire some experienced guys and get this thing fixed—quickly? I have to figure out a way to replace more than $9 million in annual sales revenue, along with more than twenty years of industry experience. That's a tough task in any industry, but especially in audiovisual and video conferencing, where there is a long learning curve and an even longer sales cycle. That's a tough combination when you're trying to get a sales team back on track.

Things were so crazy, and I sure didn't want them to get any crazier. But what if? What if they could get it done? And maybe get it done bigger and better than we had done before? Could it happen?

It's funny how things work out in a time of crisis. Some people say it builds character, but in our case, I think it revealed it. Something felt different that afternoon when Derek and I hooked up on the conference call with the rest of the ISI sales team. You could feel it. All of them were giving off the same vibe: *no fear*. Without words, they were saying, *We got you covered, boss.*

That's when I got my first clue about ISI's future, and it was not what I expected. Where I expected fear and panic in response to all the chaos on the sales team, it was actually quite the opposite. There was calm and quiet determination.

I was surprised and decided to speak first. I told them what we were dealing with.

"In the last few weeks, we lost two serious sales guys who accounted for a lot of business for the past few years. I'm not going to lie to you. It's 'go' time, and I need each of you to step up," I said. "I will do everything in my power to support you," I continued, "but this is your time to shine, and we all need to be a team and work together."

Then it was Derek's turn to speak. "I have put a lot of effort into this company for a long time, and I will be damned if I will see it go down the drain. You guys need to go out there and blaze your own trail and make your mark on ISI. I will help you in any way I can for you to be successful. Don't let me down," he concluded.

I was blown away. I always knew Derek was competitive and loyal, with all kinds of technical talent. But being inspirational? It was completely unexpected but rewarding to hear. I had never been prouder of him since I hired him back in 1997. *He is a symbol for the new ISI*, I was thinking, and I felt good about it. We were going after this most recent crisis doing what we do best: working it out as a team.

After that conference call and a nice vacation weekend with my kids and Maureen, I remembered the old saying "What doesn't kill you makes you stronger." So far, we were hurting on a lot of levels, but we were hanging in there. Another saying popped in my head: "Out of great distress comes great opportunity." We certainly had the distress, so maybe now was the time for opportunity.

One thing about baseball is that you don't just play well in high school or college and end up at the Show. (That's the term the pros use when they are called up to the major leagues.) There is a process for developing major league players called the farm system, and teams within that system are called farm teams. Wikipedia defines a farm team as "a team or club whose role is to provide experience and training for young players, with an agreement that any successful players can move on to a higher level at a given point."[2]

The farm system was actually invented by a guy named Branch Rickey, who used it to help build the great St. Louis Cardinals teams during the 1920s, '30s, and '40s. Rickey's concept was to create a constant pipeline of new talent for the Cardinals by purchasing numerous minor league ball clubs and having a chance to evaluate and grow their own talent. "From quantity comes quality," he once observed, and it worked like a charm for a long time.

The Cardinals would win nine National League pennants and six World Series championships between 1926 and 1946, proving the effectiveness of the farm system concept. Indeed, the second club to fully embrace such a system, the New York Yankees, used it to sustain their dynasty from the mid-1930s through the middle of the 1960s.[3]

The farm system allows the parent ball club to evaluate the talent that they have signed. The parent club also gets time to see the whole player, on and off the field. It's a thoughtful process that brings the players up and trains them the way they want them trained to hopefully ensure future success. It's not taking the easy way out by just signing a player and throwing them to the wolves. Players like Derek Jeter, Jorge Posada, and Mariano Rivera were products of the Yankees' farm system, and they turned out okay. Interestingly enough, since 1965, only twenty-one out of more than a thousand players have bypassed the farm system and gone directly to the

2   "Farm team," Wikipedia, http://en.wikipedia.org/wiki/Farm_team, accessed January 22, 2013.

3   "Farm team," Wikipedia, http://en.wikipedia.org/wiki/Farm_team, accessed January 22, 2013.

major leagues, a rarity for sure. And so for the vast majority of both players and ball clubs, the farm system strategy has clearly proven to be a winning formula. The farm system is also used as a metaphor for any organization or activity that serves as a training ground for higher-level endeavors. For instance, sometimes business schools are referred to as farm clubs for the world of business. It seemed logical to me as a baseball nut that to rebuild ISI's sales team, we needed to take a brand new approach—an approach that was vastly different from that of our competitors. We were going to use the farm system concept and grow our own. If it worked well for major league baseball, then why can't it work for ISI?

After that difficult summer of 2007, we had to decide what needed to happen next to get the company back on track. Clearly we needed to replace the two salespeople who left us, but what else? After being in business for more than eleven years, I was wondering if it was time to batten down the hatches and just ride this out. Or should we do something different?

Every day is so crazy and exciting and risky for a start-up business. From one day to the next, you're not sure you are even going to make it. So many times through the years, ISI was on the brink. Like back in 1996, when I drove four hours to Paducah, Kentucky, to get a check so I could make payment on our line of credit. Banks are funny about getting paid on time. Or back in 1997, when I begged a customer from a local hospital to print out a check before noon so I could make payroll that next day. Close call? You bet! Thrilling? Maybe in a sick sort of way. And we had a whopping three employees at the time!

So when we were deciding what to do in the fall of 2007, it was clear that I had to think about where I was mentally at the time. Did I still have the guts, drive, determination, or whatever you want to call it to deal with another risky move? It's interesting to see how many entrepreneurs tend to "plateau" their businesses and careers because they lose the appetite for risk. Why is that? Have they lost their ambition? Do they get comfortable just getting by? Maybe they just want to play it safe, or maybe they simply don't have the skill set to provide their company the vision for growth. Many small business owners, once their businesses mature, tend to get in a comfort zone and lose their appetite for growth and spirit for innovation. "If it ain't broke, don't fix it" becomes their mantra, which is low risk but also low reward.

Whatever the reason, I was well aware that many companies simply hit the wall at some point. But another thought occurred to me: *I wonder if we can do even better than we have done so far? Why do we have to stop now?* I began by asking myself, *Why am I doing this, anyway?* I've always said that from the beginning my goal for ISI was simple. I wanted us to "be all that we can be." Yep, just like the recruiting theme for the Army. I wanted us to reach our full potential, whatever that looked like. In trying to reach that goal, it was clear that it all started with sales. Sure, we had grown a fair amount since the start-up. We had revenue of $262,000 in our first year and a little more than $11 million in 2006. Not eye-popping stats, but certainly respectable, and we had done it all with no debt.

Unlike so many of my Inc. 500 cohorts, I was not hell-bent on growth at any cost. My plan was for more long-term, measured growth. But to do that some things would have to change, and change involved more risk.

So, I thought about developing a first-class sales team and what it would take. I could hire some industry veterans and look for a more immediate impact. In some circles they call them rainmakers. When law firms hire these kinds of people, they expect them to come "with their files." It's not a bad strategy, but not a perfect one either. What about those noncompete clauses in some employment contracts? Were they enforceable? If these folks have industry experience, do they also come with any of the bad habits associated with other employers?

And also, how do I find these people? Do I contact a headhunter? At this point, ISI had never had to use a headhunter to recruit any employee, so why start now? In the end, who knows my business and industry better than me? And what about the money? I had heard it can be really expensive, like half of the employee's first-year salary. When you look at the financials of any small business owner, what is the expense that jumps out at you? Payroll. Your employees are your biggest asset and also biggest expense. And after what I had been through the past few months, hiring employees was a sensitive subject.

But I couldn't help thinking, *You hired three good young sales guys who have gone through the ISI farm system and are starting to do pretty well. Why not just expand the farm system?*

After much deliberation and soul searching, I came to the conclusion to stick to what's been working for me, to continue to develop the ISI farm system. Identify the young talent that is out there and develop them. Build for the future and don't look for a quick fix. Stay focused and stay positive. It all sounded good, but would I execute?

So often entrepreneurs look for elaborate strategies to drive business success. But maybe the simple strategies are the best. Luckily, with everything on the line, I found the answer. It was right in front of me, and all I had to do was listen. I found my answer in Jeremy Johnson, one of ISI's key account managers who was also a guy I hired from a completely different industry. He had been with us for the last two years, and I always thought he was one of the best pure salespeople I had met in the last few years.

So, I asked Jeremy about recruiting. His response: "I think I know what it takes to be successful here, so let me make some calls and see who I can come up with." Being a young guy himself, I knew most of Jeremy's contacts would be of the Millennial generation, but recruiting young people was the logical way to build the ISI farm system.

As we rebuilt the ISI sales team, we also added personnel to support our vertical market niches, most profitable products, and biggest accounts. I remember a good customer of ours stated at the time, "Jay, it's not that complicated—stick to what you're good at."

One area ISI was good at that I particularly wanted to improve was our contract support for distance learning and audio visual equipment with the community colleges and higher learning institutions in the state. Our contract had been in place for a number of years and was worth millions of dollars annually, yet we continued to provide only part-time support. In other words, we weren't focusing on one of our bread-and-butter vertical market niches, and that was simply not smart business. So we decided to add a sales guy to focus specifically on the education market. Simple stuff, really. Take care of your customers and they will take care of you.

Another simple strategy occurred to me, something I had been thinking about for some time. Besides focusing a sales guy on our biggest vertical market with education, why not focus someone on the company's most profitable product? ISI's most profitable product actually wasn't a product at all. Like many businesses in other industries, our service and maintenance contracts had the best profit margins. Look at how car dealers make money. They typically make a little money when they sell the cars, but most of the profit is in the service department. ISI was no different.

Besides the profitability side of it, what about the practical side of selling service and maintenance contracts? Customers who buy our equipment want it to work properly every day, and when it doesn't, they need assistance. If ISI didn't provide that assistance, then some other company would, and that could create big problems for us. Entrepreneurs have to protect their customer base every day and never, ever take it for granted. In looking at our customer base, not only did they have service needs, but revenue from repeat customers accounted for more than 75 percent of ISI's annual revenue year after year. Focus a guy on selling maintenance contracts? You bet! This wasn't just for company profitability, but to ensure another year of survival. And that was a good thing.

Sticking to our farm system strategy, we recruited salespeople from all areas. Our guy who handles our educational markets, Kyle Yates, had a background in selling specialty advertising items— things like key chains, squeeze balls, and coffee cups. It might not have been very high tech, but it required him to make a ton of calls and be good with details, making him an ideal fit for ISI's educational customers.

And for the maintenance and service salesperson? How about a guy who used to repossess cars? In his prior job, our services account manager, Josh Wilbanks, would make calls every day to people who had not made their car payments and tell them he was picking up their car. What a grind! When we hired Josh, he was happy to get a job where people weren't cussing him out or hanging up on him (or both) every day.

So Josh had pretty tough skin, but he was also very good with numbers and pretty low key with the sales process. The fact that he wasn't a high-pressure salesperson made him a perfect fit for ISI's maintenance customers. Like most of us, many of our clients love to buy stuff; they just don't like the feeling of being sold to. Here's the bottom line in evaluating talent in the farm system: Many times you need to look beyond the resume. It's not so much what a candidate has done, but what they can do in the future. Look inside their heart, and that will tell you what they are made of.

So we had addressed our most important vertical and our most profitable product and service by assigning a sales guy to each market. Now we turned our attention to major accounts. Outside of education, ISI's business model focused on selling to a number of Fortune 500 customers that had opportunity for growth. But they needed focus and attention. So it wasn't hard to figure out what we needed to do next: have someone focus on major accounts and grow the business.

And the last piece of the sales strategy puzzle? ISI Nashville had been in place since 2005, yet we had never really grown that office to the degree we thought we could. Obviously, Nashville was not just any remote location. It is the home of country music, state government, and many Fortune 500 companies in manufacturing, health care, and more. In fact, the Nashville region is home to more than 1.5 million people and 40,000 businesses. Nashville's advantages have attracted more diverse new business from across the country than any city its size over the past twenty years. Due to this success, Nashville has become a who's who of corporate relocations, home to headquarters offices of HCA, Asurion, Bridgestone Americas, Nissan North America, and more. Clearly this was an area of future growth for ISI's business, so we decided it was time to get serious about Nashville or get out.

But what was the best way to grow our business in Nashville and focus a guy on major accounts? Lots of options and some made more sense than others. In the end it was really pretty easy. Rather than hire an unknown sales guy and put him in such an important market, we decided to relocate our strongest sales guy from Memphis, Michael Sanders, and have him sell into major accounts and energize the local Nashville market. Kill 2 birds with one stone. It made sense for both

ISI and Michael. He was looking for a change in scenery, and we needed someone to help grow an important part of our territory. And it was the farm system that allowed us to spare him and grow our business in ways we otherwise could not.

Yes, relying on unproven talent to grow the business was risky. But if my goal was to avoid risk, my only other option was to stand around and hope we'd grow. That reminds me of another saying: Hope is not a strategy. That's the thing about being an entrepreneur and owning a mature business that needs to grow. You can't get conservative and stop taking risks. In essence, you have to believe in yourself.

That was the game plan. It wasn't brain surgery, just executing business fundamentals. Hire quality personnel and have them focus on profitable niches that need additional sales support.

ISI had recruited these new sales guys to help grow the company and launch us into the future. But exactly how were they going to do that? This is another simple but important part of growing a sustainable business. We had to train these new guys. None of them knew anything about video conferencing or audiovisual technology, so we had to teach them.

Training is an area where you should never try to cut corners to save money. If you ask your salespeople (or any other personnel for that matter) to go out and do the job, to sell millions of dollars in product, you have to equip them to do so. And this doesn't mean hand them a brochure or have them spend a day traveling with a service tech. It means spending money on professional training programs offered by manufacturers and others. In high tech, it means investing in demonstration equipment and high-speed networks. It means investing in your people so that they can produce for you. And it needs to be a constant.

At ISI, we firmly believe in continuous education, so we invite our suppliers, vendors, and partners to come by our office to update our people on new products or strategies. We also encourage our people to read industry publications and any related technical material that will help increase their product knowledge. That goes to the core of ISI's beliefs and approach to the marketplace: We don't want people to just sell or support our products. We want our folks to be a resource for our clients and help them with whatever needs they may have related to technology. That doesn't limit itself to just video conferencing or audiovisual technology. We want our clients to call us and seek information on whatever technology needs they may have and see the ISI account manager as their technology consultant.

From our perspective, we want the ISI brand not to be just a video conferencing and audiovisual integrator, but an emerging technology firm on the leading edge of new trends and products in a wide array of technologies. We are more like a partner to our clients, not just a hardware or software vendor (which I'll expand more on later).

So we invested in ourselves that fall of 2007, both emotionally and financially. It was hard for me to pick up the pieces from the tumultuous summer, but I did. As conservative as I am, I resigned myself to the fact that you have to spend money to make money, another old adage I have heard through the years. It was hard to do, but in the end, it was that simple.

In general, it is virtually impossible to be successful in business without knowing who you are, identifying a specific product offering, and developing a go-to-market strategy. So as we reorganized and expanded the sales team, we also took the opportunity to clearly define who we were and what our brand was by creating a mission statement. As corny as it sounds, creating a mission statement is important for a number of reasons, if for no other reason than to make sure everyone is singing off the same song sheet. It was wonderful to reorganize the company in late 2007, but we needed to make sure we were pointing the company in the right direction.

It's funny how often we assume everyone knows and understands this concept, and how many times it's just not true. At our kickoff meeting in 2008, we asked the sales team to write up what they believed to be our mission statement. Eight different guys wrote an answer on a piece of paper. And guess what we got back? You got it: eight different answers to the question. Were we on the same song sheet? Hell, we weren't even in the same book. But that's the point: You have to make sure you have defined yourself as an organization. Just as you cannot ask salespeople to sell a product that they don't really know, you also can't have people telling all sorts of different stories about your company's purpose or capabilities. So at that meeting, together we reworked the wording of the mission statement to more clearly reflect the company brand. Here was the result: "ISI's mission is to provide high-quality video conferencing and audiovisual solutions to all our clients with above and beyond service and support on a daily basis."

Short and sweet, but it got the job done.

It was amazing how energized and fired up everyone was about 2008. I just watched and took it all in with sheer amazement. Wasn't it just a few months ago that the world felt like it was falling apart? That sick feeling in my stomach I had for months had been replaced with a different feeling, a feeling of excitement that I hadn't felt in quite a while. It was a sense that brighter days were ahead. "Out of the ashes rises the phoenix." Maybe this was just what the company needed to move forward.

ISI had new people, a carefully constructed sales strategy, and a positive attitude for growth. As best we could figure, we had made all the right moves since the major turnover crisis that summer. Ironically, just when we started to get the ISI house in order, there was a much larger obstacle on the horizon. It was one over which we had no control, but it was destined to change the course of our business and thousands of others for many years to come.

Three words: *the Great Recession.*

Stepping Up to the Plate

Key ways your business can use turnover to inspire fresh ways of doing business:

1. **Be receptive to change.** So many mature businesses get complacent and believe that if they make changes or take risks, they may lose it all. For ISI, it took a major shakeup to realize we needed to take a fresh new approach to growing the business.

2. **Dare to be different.** Implementing the farm system approach to building the ISI sales team was just one way to think differently and more strategically about the business. In not looking for just a quick fix, ISI sent the message to not only the sales team but also the rest of the company that we were in it for the long haul, and we were going to do it right. We also chose rebuilding the sales team as the impetus to work on changing the rest of the company for the better.

3. **Train your team, leveraging all the professional resources you can assemble.** Do not skimp here, and it will pay dividends.

4. **Develop a clear mission statement, and make sure everyone understands it and supports it.**

CHAPTER 3

CHOOSING NOT TO PARTICIPATE IN A RECESSION

Wikipedia defines a recession as "a business cycle contraction, a general slowdown in economic activity. Macroeconomic indicators such as GDP, employment, investment spending, capacity utilization, household income, business profits, and inflation fall, while bankruptcies and the unemployment rate rise. Recessions generally occur when there is a widespread drop in spending (an adverse demand shock). This may be triggered by various events, such as a financial crisis, an external trade shock, an adverse supply shock, or bursting of an economic bubble. Governments usually respond to recessions by adopting expansionary macroeconomic policies, such as increasing money supply, increasing government spending, and decreasing taxation . . . Some economists prefer a definition of a 1.5 percent rise in unemployment within twelve months."[4]

However you define it, it was certainly not the most ideal time to expand the ISI sales team and add to the company overhead numbers. I'm not going to lie and say that I didn't recognize the warning signs out there. But on the other hand, what do you do as a business? Sure, it's scary to turn on the TV or radio and hear about all the growing economic problems. What if I made a mistake hiring all these people? What if they don't work out? What if I take on too much overhead and run the company into the ground?

Entrepreneurs are generally optimists by nature, and I would definitely put myself in that category. But, more important, ISI and I have survived because I am also a realist. Fortunately, through the years I have been able to get a sense of the right direction for the company to take, and it's worked out. But the mind can play some crazy tricks on you, particularly when you have no control over the situation. And as a business owner, when you start doubting yourself, you're in trouble. Doubt can definitely be a nasty enemy. But realistically, our options were either to stay the course or to freeze in fear. Which is better for your business?

It seemed like everyone was very cautious at the start of 2008, and ISI was no different. We got our new sales team in place, trained them as quickly as possible, focused on our strong market niches, and tried to block everything else out. But another very simple strategy we had, which yielded powerful results, was to begin holding regular company meetings—or, as one of our employees called it, Jay's Dance Party. The meetings were companywide and connected through audio and video conferencing so that all employees could

---

4   "Recession," Wikipedia, http://en.wikipedia.org/wiki/Recession, accessed
     February 1, 2013.

participate, even if they were on the road or at a customer site. The company bought everyone's lunch, the agenda would include a few topics to discuss, and then we would open the meeting up for questions or comments.

The questions ran the gamut. We got general questions, like "Where is the company going in the future?" And we got trickier questions, like "How is the recession going to affect ISI?" I'm not sure that I answered every question perfectly, but that's not really the point. The point was that as the owner of ISI, I wanted to communicate that we were all in it together and that I was in the boat with them.

I also wanted to communicate that, as their leader, I was going to continue to be as transparent as possible in all of my decisions and strategies related to the company's future. More than ever before, with so many other companies in the country exhibiting deceptive and unethical behavior, I was going to make sure my employees did not get fed the company line. Whether it was good, bad, or otherwise, I was going to tell them the truth. I wanted them to know I wasn't Bernie Madoff or Allen Stanford, and I wasn't going to tell them one thing while being totally unethical behind closed doors. I'm also a board member of the Better Business Bureau, and I am very proud of the values that organization promotes in business. Honesty and integrity is my personal brand.

In addition to honesty and integrity, I also made sure that I was communicating and instilling confidence in the company's direction. They certainly didn't need to hear any nervousness or uncertainty. So, overall, my strategy was to realistically evaluate where the company was going and deliver the message with a positive attitude. Was there anything else I needed to communicate?

Well, maybe it's the competitor in me, or my pride, or plain stubbornness, but there was something else I repeated in 2008 over and over again. Here it is: *"ISI is choosing not to participate in the recession."*

I really believed that. We were going to navigate these difficult times and we were going to come out bigger and better for it. That was just the way it was going to be. No excuses. No uncertainty. I just kept reiterating the clear direction of my vision for ISI. It's amazing how employees react when they have leaders who believe in them. From 2008 going forward, we all knew we would need strong leadership to get through the coming days.

This was no small feat and was not going to be a "quick fix." The recession of 2007 was unlike any other in recent memory, and many compared it to the Great Depression of the 1930s. It began in 2007 when sky-high home prices in the United States took an unexpected turn and went decisively downward and quickly. It was like a fast-spreading disease: first to the entire US financial sector and then to financial markets overseas. The casualties in the United States included the entire investment banking industry, the biggest insurance company in the nation, the two enterprises chartered by the government to facilitate mortgage lending, the largest mortgage lender in the nation, the largest savings and loan, and two of the largest commercial banks.[5]

Companies that normally rely on credit suffered heavily as well, like the American auto industry. Banks, trusting no one to pay them back (including small business owners) simply stopped making the loans that most businesses needed to regulate their cash flows and without which they cannot do business. Share prices plunged throughout the world—the Dow Jones Industrial Average in the United States lost 33.8 percent of its value in 2008—and by the end of the year, a deep recession had enveloped most of the globe.[6] Sure made for many sleepless nights in 2008.

---

5   "The Financial Crisis of 2008: Year in Review 2008," Encyclopaedia Britannica, http://www.britannica.com/EBchecked/topic/1484264/The-Financial-Crisis-of-2008-Year-In-Review-2008

6   Ibid.

It was beyond scary, and ISI was trying to grow a business in this environment. Yet there was another thing we decided that year at ISI that was perhaps the biggest key to our success. We decided that, although we were sympathetic to all the businesses and industries that were going through hard times, we had to consciously focus on who we were as a company. We had to remind ourselves that ISI wasn't a bank and didn't sell subprime mortgages, and many of those issues creating the economic crisis had nothing to do with us. We focused on our brand and our value proposition. ISI is a technology company that sells products and services that, in many cases, save businesses thousands of dollars every day in travel expenses and increase employee productivity. That's in essence who we are and what we do.

We also decided that there was never a better time to buy our technology, because when times are tough, businesses will need ISI technology to help make them more efficient and productive. We created a positive spin to navigate a negative environment.

And it worked! As we pressed on through the year, 2008 was really shaping up to be a record-setting sales year. It was crazy, but with a group of mostly rookie salespeople, ISI was going to grow the business from $11.5 million in sales to more than $14.5 million. This was an incredible performance, considering the worldwide economic conditions. Had we seen the worst yet? We certainly hoped so.

Stepping Up **to the Plate**

Key points to remember about how to choose not to participate in a recession:

1. **Communicate frequently and transparently.** Whether you choose to have town meetings like ISI did or other forms of companywide events, make all communication with employees open and transparent. Being honest and up-front with employees will go a long way to encourage loyalty and dedication in the current skeptical business environment.

2. **Lead with confidence.** It's critical that you as a leader communicate a clear vision of the future with confidence to your employees. A confident leader who paints a picture of future success to his employees will motivate them to work hard to achieve it.

3. **Believe in your people.** Although small business ownership is highly personal, keep in mind that many of your employees have a vested interest in the success of the business as well. This is particularly true of your tenured employees, who many times are as invested as you are in your business.

CHAPTER 4

USE YOUR BOOK
AS YOUR HOOK

I remember October 18, 2007, like it was yesterday. It was the launch party for my first book, *Keep Swinging: An Entrepreneur's Story of Overcoming Adversity and Achieving Small Business Success* (Morgan James, 2007). We were all gathered at AutoZone Park, where the Memphis Redbirds play baseball and a venue for a variety of other events, such as rock concerts and fireworks shows. With the picture of a guy (not me) swinging a baseball bat on the front cover and baseball as the book's metaphor, it made total sense to have the kickoff at a ballpark.

As I looked around from the founders' suite, high above the playing field, I saw about forty or fifty people there to celebrate my book getting published, which was very gratifying for me. It was also a welcome break for ISI employees, who had to endure all the upheaval within the company for the past few months. They certainly needed a nice night out. In addition to giving out copies of the book to all of my employees, I was also hoping I could twist a few arms and get some family and friends to buy a few copies, maybe just to humor me. I really had no goals for the book other than that.

Book Launch Party, October 2007. *It's still crazy to think about all the places that* Keep Swinging *has taken me over the past five years.*

Even after all the effort that went into getting it published, it certainly wasn't my goal to be another John Grisham, sell millions of copies of my book, and become famous. Also, as a first-time author, I knew that the numbers weren't pretty. The number of books being published every year had exploded: The number of new print titles issued by US publishers has grown from 215,777 in 2002 to 411,422 in 2007,[7] and from 2007 to 2010 more than 2.7 million nontraditional titles were projected to be published, including self-published books, reprints of public domain works, and print-on-demand books. In addition, hundreds of thousands of English-language books are published each year outside the United States. And here are the numbers that really hit home to me. The average US nonfiction book sells fewer than 250 copies per year.[8]

To make matters even that much more challenging, a book has less than a 1 percent chance of being stocked in an average bookstore. One hundred to 1,000 or more titles compete for every spot on a bookstore's shelf. For example, the number of business titles stocked ranges from fewer than 100 (in the smaller bookstores) to approximately 1,500 (in the superstores). Yet there are more than 250,000 business books in print fighting for that limited shelf space. And to top it off, only 62 of 1,000 business books have sold more than 5,000 copies. With those daunting statistics in front of me, I remember asking myself, *What the hell am I doing? Why did I come up with this crazy idea to write a book? Have I gone off the deep end?* Maybe I had, and after people read my book, that fact would be confirmed.

On the other hand, I wanted to get *Keep Swinging* out to as many readers as I could. Why couldn't my book be one of the chosen few sold in Barnes and Noble, the largest bookstore in the country at the time? Nothing like dreaming big. That's what I preach to my kids and my employees: You have to dream big to make big things happen. Right?

I also believed it was a pretty good book. I majored in marketing in school, I spent a lot of time on it, and I think it's pretty well written. Plus, it's different. *Keep Swinging* isn't a bunch of canned advice with graphs and charts typical of most business books. It was emotional,

---

7   Source: www.bowker.com.
8   BJ Gallagher, "The Ten Awful Truths—and the Ten Wonderful Truths—about Book Publishing," *Huffington Post*, April 5, 2012.

loaded with very personal stories and advice, with a dose of inspiration thrown in as well. It just might have a pretty big audience—it might even save a few businesses from bankruptcy if they read the chapter on embezzlement. But how would I get it out there? Who would I get it to? And how could it help ISI?

After putting a lot of thought into it, I came to the conclusion that there had to be a way to use my book differently, not just to promote me as an author, but also as more of a marketing tool for ISI. I decided to use *Keep Swinging* as a unique company brochure of sorts and viewed it as a platform to help grow ISI's business. This was a way we could look different from our competition and truly set ourselves apart. Of course, I had no idea exactly how that would work. I'm in the technology business—people in my industry don't read many books, much less write them. Writing a book and thus becoming an author was one thing. But leveraging that to grow my technology business—in 2007, at the start of the Great Recession? Even for an optimist like me, that was a big leap of faith.

But it's funny—even at the book launch at AutoZone Park that night, I got a sense that getting my book published was going to take me and ISI to some new places, places we never thought about before. It was exciting to just think of the possibilities. As the party wound down and I got a chance to take it all in, a friend came by and asked me, "Think you'll sell many copies of your book?" I paused and replied, "Sure hope so." All of a sudden, I thought, *I'm a nobody. I'll be lucky if I sell a hundred copies, or maybe hit that average number. What was it, 250 copies?* I was just hoping I wouldn't make a total fool of myself.

Because even though I wasn't in it to become a famous author, before I could implement a new strategy for using the book, I still needed to see what people thought of it. I needed validation that my book had value before I took the next steps toward using it to promote my business. I could have put in a whole lot of effort for some very small results. That's the thing about writing a book: You never really know what people will think of it, or whether it will sell or not.

That validation came shortly after the book came out, when I got my first book review on About.com.

> Keep Swinging *is a little different than most books on this topic because Myers shies away from explaining all of his good decisions and instead focuses on some of the mistakes he has made and the pitfalls he has faced. Stories of a poor business plan, a misguided buyout, and an embezzlement crisis all blend together to create a compelling tale that reads more like a fiction book.*
>
> *At the same time,* Keep Swinging *offers solid business lessons and advice that any entrepreneurs could put to good use. Myers also touches on subjects like home life, family support, continuing education, and community involvement.*
>
> *The book is only 157 pages, but it includes a lot of valuable information and entertainment value to boot. I would highly recommend* Keep Swinging *to any entrepreneur who wants to read about both the highs and lows of owning a business.*[9]

The review blew me away. The reviewer said she liked my book. It didn't suck. That's good, I thought. And the only critique was that it was too short? That's not too shabby. My book seemed to have struck a chord with people, and that made me feel good. As days and weeks went by, the book gained momentum, and that's when I started getting the emails and personal notes from readers.

One person who was going through some recent hard times emailed me and said that my book "helped them get through the day"

---

9   Karen Schweitzer, "Keep Swinging," About.com, http://businessmajors.about.com/od/booksonleadership/gr/KeepSwinging.htm.

and thanked me for writing it. A short time later, after one of my first speeches about the book at the Collierville Chamber of Commerce, I got an email from a local businessman who was in attendance that day. He went home and read the book in one night! He was so enthusiastic that he wrote me an email at two a.m. and told me how much he loved the book and the various advice he had picked up that would help him in his new business. He then ordered twenty-five books that he was going to sell out of his computer store and spread the word of *Keep Swinging* for me.

Are you kidding me? This couldn't be happening. I wrote that book just to tell a few stories, but now people were getting real value out of it. But indeed it was happening, and it was only the beginning. A few days later, another reader wrote, "Congratulations for your inspirational story, especially for all the budding entrepreneurs out there working to build their business." One reader even wrote, "Just finished reading *Keep Swinging* at 3:48 a.m. It's already been a great inspiration!"

Wow! We were off to a great start, but I was still conflicted about what we could do with it. Personally, I wanted to somehow use it to help me turn the page on a number of my difficult personal experiences. Writing it was a form of catharsis, and sharing these stories might help me heal wounds from my past. I also wanted to share some stories about what had happened to me, to my family, and to my business. I wanted to share the stories of our struggles and our triumphs. I wanted to talk about all the obstacles that we had to overcome through the years. I wanted people to know that starting a business is not easy and keeping it going is even harder.

I also wanted people to know small business is personal and that sometimes it's hard to separate the two. I wanted people to know more about me and my business, how we got started and how we got to where we are today. I wanted to let people know that I didn't come from money and that I built the business the old-fashioned way, with *hard work*. In essence, I wanted to bare my soul. But I really didn't expect the effect it would have on me personally and professionally. The experience was already so rewarding. But the specific *value* of using my book as a marketing hook to grow ISI's business was beginning to emerge even though I was still a little unsure about the concept.

In truth, my publisher, David Hancock at Morgan James Publishing, had already explained the concept of using your book as your marketing hook to me, but I must have been a little slow in understanding how it all worked. David is a former mortgage banker who told me he increased his business significantly after he wrote his first book, using his book as a platform for branding him as a subject matter expert. David noticed that when he gave various speeches and presentations, people treated him differently when it was revealed that he was a published author. He was treated like a rock star and was looked upon as a guy who really knew his stuff. David decided to create a new publishing business model around his experience.

Through Morgan James Publishing, David's goal was to create a niche of entrepreneurial authors who maintain their day jobs but write books to help grow their businesses. Becoming a published author carries a certain amount of prestige, which is fun and exciting, but David encourages the practical side of it. Use your book as a platform to make more money for you and your company.

But for me, the question was, How do you do that in the technology industry? After the initial buzz about the book, I sat down with David and his colleagues to decide what I wanted to do next. Many ideas were kicked around, but the one thing I decided that had to happen was to make sure we got the word out to as many people as we could.

So I signed up with a public relations company called Planned Television Arts (PTA, now Media Connect) out of New York City that helped me shape a campaign for *Keep Swinging*. PTA helped create a national audience for *Keep Swinging* that I couldn't possibly reach otherwise. It was money well spent, because PTA helped position my book nationally and achieve instant credibility. This allowed us to not only do radio interviews all across the country but also schedule book signing events at major bookstore locations such as Barnes and Noble in Memphis, Nashville, Chicago, and others. In addition, PTA's radio tour campaign had my book and ISI's name broadcast coast to coast

Book Signing at Barnes and Noble/Chicago. *It's great to meet fans of* Keep Swinging *in all parts of the country.*

for several weeks in prime drive time with maximum listenership, which was priceless publicity and a lot of fun.

After the initial PR campaign concluded with a TV appearance on Fox Business and an article in the Huffington Post, we thought more about the message of the book and who it might appeal to. And we were still thinking, *How does the book help grow ISI's business? What's the return on investment?* Initially our thoughts on marketing were focused on start-up entrepreneurs and small business owners who represent a very large but highly fragmented market. We had forged some great relationships with the small business community as a result of the exposure that the book was getting. In fact, with the success of *Keep Swinging*, I had become a regular guest on the nationally syndicated *Small Business Advocate* radio show with Jim Blasingame (www.smallbusinessadvocate.com). Jim is widely considered to be one of the world's foremost experts on small business and entrepreneurship—not a bad guy to get to know, and a person who has generously provided some really good advice to me both personally and professionally through the years.

But were there other sales prospects we could reach? Maybe not a direct return through book sales, but something else? What else could we do with the book to justify the time I've put into it and help ISI grow? Then it came to me: *Who really needs to read the book for it to have the biggest impact on ISI?* It was stupid simple. How about the people that are paying the bills for the company—the people we count on every day to support our livelihood? Why not send a copy of the book to every ISI client and prospect? We could enclose a letter that tells them how much we value their interest in our company and that the enclosed book was a small token of appreciation for doing business with ISI. We would explain that the book outlines a number of things about the history of the company, the ups and downs through the years, and the value system that we are based on. Clients always like to receive gifts in the mail, and this may be one they really get a kick out of.

Why not reveal ourselves to our clients, the very lifeline of our business and the ones who will appreciate it the most? It made so much sense. More than that, it was different. None of us knew of any supplier or competitor that had done anything like this. No one had written a book, much less was sending one out as a gift to their clients. So that's what we started doing in 2008, after the book started to gain some sales momentum.

We created a new audience for the book, an audience that could not only justify the time I spent on the book, but perhaps stimulate even more growth with existing clients. We were going to send the letter to every ISI client, prospect, supplier, friend of the firm, and so on. We were going to tell our story to the world via *Keep Swinging*. It was worth a try. The following is the letter that everybody received with a copy of the book.

Dear ISI Customer:

I want to take this opportunity to personally thank you for your continued business relationship with Interactive Solutions, Inc. (ISI). ISI would not be able to enjoy the success that we have today without valued customer relationships such as the one we have with you. You folks are the best!

As a small token of appreciation, I am enclosing a copy of my first book that was recently published, titled Keep Swinging: An Entrepreneur's Story of Overcoming Adversity and Achieving Small Business Success (www. keepswingingbook.com).

So you know, I wrote this book as a means of providing some hope and inspiration to struggling small business owners and as a means of showing gratitude for being able to overcome many obstacles through the past several years. It has been quite a ride.

Also, as an ISI customer, I hope the book will give you a keener insight into the kind of company you have chosen to invest in and the value system that drives all of us.

Once again, thanks for the continued business and enjoy the book. If I can ever be of assistance, please call me directly at 901-866-1474 or email me at jmyers@isitn.com.

Sincerely,
Jay B. Myers
Founder/ CEO
Interactive Solutions, Inc.

Winning the 2010 Ethan Award. *One of the biggest thrills of my professional career (with my publisher, David Hancock, in Las Vegas).*

The letter was pretty straightforward and to the point, but our clients told us that it was really something different. None of their other vendors had ever treated them like this. It was unique, and they liked it. Apparently people still really enjoy an all-American success story, and ISI qualified as one of them. We were all very humbled by the whole notion of that, especially me.

And then a funny thing happened as we were sending out the books and letters. The 2008 sales revenue kept increasing every month. Every month I was receiving a nice email or handwritten note from an ISI client, expressing appreciation for the book and its inspiring message, and we kept getting more.

Here's a sample of the feedback from the letters and books we sent out.

I thank you most sincerely for your book (which I finished reading over the weekend). It was like a spy novel, a business case study, and a life lessons type of aggregation all rolled up into one well-written little package.

It was very enjoyable reading and reminded me of several friends I have made through the years who have all come from the sales business. I now have even greater admiration for you and your company, as well as the folks who work for you and have stuck by you through thick and thin.

Your book is quite inspirational. It encourages all of us to dig a little deeper at times and think about the challenge of overcoming the trust of a dishonest employee, the importance of the role your spouse played, and of course, your health being challenged midstream. It's the stories that legends are made from.

Most of these messages were sent via email, but many others were handwritten notes that took time to write. It was a simple gesture to send out a book and thank them for their business, but I think revealing ourselves through the stories in the book gave our clients a deeper understanding of who we are, where we came from, and our value system. Was it that revolutionary? Not really. But with the world spinning out of control in 2008, and with all the economic and corporate woes, *Keep Swinging* seemed to be the kind of tonic people were looking for.

The book brought out feelings about ISI that a company brochure with standard propaganda could not possibly achieve. And the sales kept coming. Reflecting back on it, as tough as 2007 was with all the personal and professional challenges, 2008 was going to be a lot different. Was it because we sent books to our clients and prospects? Was it because the book was so personal and they learned so much about me and the company? Was it because they liked the message? Was it because they liked our value system and how we run the business?

To this day I'm not 100 percent sure of exactly why things happened the way they did except to say that these are the facts. After *Keep Swinging* was published in October 2007, ISI did in fact immediately increase revenue from $11 million in 2007 to more than $14.5 million in 2008 despite dealing with the global economic crisis (like everyone else). We not only increased our top line revenue number by almost 32 percent but also increased our profit margins as well. Was it an accident? Or was it pure luck? Or maybe ISI's prospect and client base responded to something new?

And maybe that's the point: ISI and I decided to take a unique approach to grow the business. We didn't try to go out and do things the same old way. Isn't that the definition of insanity, doing the same thing over and over again and expecting different results?

We also chose to grow the old-fashioned way, which made sense to me: one customer at a time. We consciously chose not to go out and try to buy a company and go into debt to grow, much like many of my Inc. 500 buddies do over and over again. Not at ISI. We stuck to our guns and chose to grow our business organically, from within our client and prospect base, and we did it with hard work combined with a unique approach.

So what happened after that? What else have we done with the book to help grow ISI's business? In 2009, we continued to send out books and letters to ISI clients and prospects but also added additional speaking engagements to help further promote and sell the book and ISI. I must say that adding this dimension to the *Keep Swinging* marketing plan has had a dramatic impact on not just book sales but also ISI's reach into additional markets. I will also say that getting in front of a large group of people to deliver your company's message is one of the most impactful marketing strategies any company can have. That is true whether or not your company is on the Fortune 500 or Inc. 5000 list.

Over the past few years, the message of *Keep Swinging* has been delivered in major markets like Chicago at DePaul University business school as well as the Collegiate Entrepreneurs' Organization and numerous other colleges and universities such as Oklahoma State University, Emory University, Belmont University, the University of Mississippi, the University of Memphis, and the University of Tennessee. In addition to the college and university marketplace, speeches were given at numerous civic, community, and industry organizations such as the Inc. 500 Conference, Kiwanis, Rotary, Leadership Collierville, Leadership Bartlett, National Systems Contractors Association, PSA Security, as well as Small Business Development Centers.

It has been rewarding to promote ISI at a very high level using the book as the platform to carry a message that is inspiring to both students and faculty. And the other added benefit? These same colleges and universities that are hosting my presentations are key ISI clients and account for more than 40 percent of ISI's revenue year in and year out. Has there been a method behind my madness? You bet! And it continues to this day. I was told numerous times by college and university faculty that they particularly appreciated the fact that I didn't have an angle when I came in as guest speaker and was there to simply convey a message to their students. More than a few commented they really felt like I was of great help in providing guidance for their students' future careers. For me, I felt my role was also there to tell them the real story behind entrepreneurship, having experienced it firsthand for many years. I think telling about life in the trenches is another way of giving back to the entrepreneurial community.

And that's another cool thing about getting a book published. It has allowed me to accomplish a couple of goals. First, I have used my book as a hook to grow ISI's business and solidify the client base, but I was also able to use it, in some small way, to improve people's lives and hopefully make a difference as well. Interestingly enough, once we determined what our message was, it became easier to promote the book to a receptive audience.

Finally, in thinking through the whole aspect of using your book as your hook, my advice is to make sure you realistically look at what a business book really is. In my opinion, it's really just a big business card. Yep, that's right. It's really just a means of introduction, and you should think of it that way. Some successful authors today have gone on the record as saying that writing a book to grow your business is a bad thing, as if that implies the book won't be valuable in and of itself. But I don't agree. If your book is going to be an effective business card, it needs to have value in and of itself. A poorly written book is no better than brochure propaganda. But the truth is that if your book really does have value, viewing it as a big business card doesn't decrease the value of your book; it increases it.

It took me a little while to figure out that business books aren't novels. They are valuable tools that can educate the world about the value of your services and thus promote business to the people you're in business to serve. I never leave town without a copy or two of *Keep Swinging* in my backpack. Why? You never know who you will meet along the way, and I truly believe that my book represents ISI better than anything I can do or say. And it's amazing some of the great comments I have gotten from people who have gotten the book. I remember giving a copy to the president of Tandberg, Inc. (now part of Cisco Systems), who has been ISI's largest supplier since the company started. He liked the book so much he ordered twenty-five copies to distribute to all of his regional vice presidents. He told me he loved the fact that one of his resellers was a published author and really like my book's message. Not a bad guy to have on your side, right?

Writing a book and getting it published can give you even more opportunities. Two of my favorite stories of additional opportunities that came my way after *Keep Swinging* was published are both sports-related, and they involve my favorite college basketball team (the Memphis Tigers) and my favorite baseball team, which is, of course, the New York Yankees.

In October 2010, I was contacted by one of the Memphis assistant coaches, who asked me to come out and speak to the team about my book and my experiences in overcoming adversity. Wow, how cool is that? I was both excited and flattered at the same time. You see, in Memphis, Tennessee, the University of Memphis basketball team is not just the local college team, they are the city's team and are treated like rock stars. So getting a chance to present to them was a *big* deal!

I can honestly say I have never had more fun doing a presentation. I remember the players not only getting a kick out of my story but also being emotionally engaged from start to finish. Afterward we exchanged autographs with each other; they all signed a basketball for me and I signed copies of *Keep Swinging* for them. As I was driving home that afternoon, I was thinking about how my book had opened up so many unbelievable opportunities for both ISI and myself personally. I've been so fortunate—it couldn't get any better than this. Or could it?

Just a short month later, in November 2010, I was down in Tampa, Florida, for the New York Yankees Fantasy Camp, another fun opportunity to play the game I love with some of the legends of the game, including former Yankees like Chris Chambliss, Jesse Barfield, Fritz Peterson, and Al Downing. This was my third camp in four years, so I decided to make this one special by donating a copy of Keep Swinging to my fellow campers, the Yankee legends, and the Fantasy Camp staff. It was just a small token of appreciation to the people who have meant so much to me the past few years—the people who for one week a year made me feel like that twelve-year-old Little Leaguer again, the one who used to lay out his uniform the day before a game and prayed it wouldn't rain.

Once I coordinated everything with the camp director, the books were placed in everyone's locker a few days after the start of the camp. Admittedly, I really wasn't sure what kind of reaction I was going to get. Would they understand? I was just hoping they would at least read the last chapter and get a kick out of the comments I made about my first Fantasy Camp experience in 2007.

A few days later, a Yankee staff member came up to me and said, "Great book, I couldn't put it down." Still another person said, "I read it in one afternoon and loved it." I was flabbergasted (and flattered). Later on I was in the bus coming back from the ballpark, and Yankee legend Al Downing came up to me and said, "Nice job with the book." I almost fell out of my seat. Later, Jesse Barfield also told me how much he liked the book and even handed me an autographed ball that was signed "Keep Swinging My Friend." Fritz Peterson enjoyed it as well and made it a point to send me a copy of his book, *Mickey Mantle Is Going to Heaven*. What a special experience to have former Yankee ballplayers reading and enjoying my book—and finding myself in yet another place my book had taken me that I would never have dreamed possible.

Also, as a result of the book, I made numerous TV appearances on the local CBS affiliate, as well as in segments on the *First Business* show in Chicago and Fox Business. The interesting thing was that I was invited on not because I'm the owner of an Inc. 500 technology company, but because I'm a published author. Put simply, a book can take you to places you can't get to any other way. Many radio and TV stations simply like sharing a human interest story on the air for wider appeal to their audience.

And speaking of taking us to places we never could be without the book, without a doubt the most rewarding experience was when *Keep Swinging* was displayed on the huge NASDAQ board in Times Square in New York City in October 2010 for having made the Inc./800CEORead best-seller list six times in a row. It doesn't get any better than that! When we got the email from the PR company with the picture attached, my son, Jordan, thought that I had gotten fancy with Photoshop and done it myself. It was crazy to see my company and book being advertised on the busiest street in the biggest city in

***Keep Swinging* on Times Square**. *It's still unreal to think my book made it to the Big Board in New York City.*

the country. It was beyond my wildest dreams, and I have to say it was also very cool! Again, I couldn't pay for that kind or publicity if I were simply trying to promote ISI or our various technology products. Something about being a successful author strikes the right chord in media marketing and appeals to a much wider audience than typical advertising for technology products.

One of the unique opportunities that the book has given me and ISI came in the form of a book review from a guy named Matti Copeland, who lives in Finland. It seems that he saw the Inc./800CEORead list and noticed that my book had been selling pretty well, and he wanted to see what it was all about.

After sending him a copy of the book and talking to him on the phone for more than an hour, the next thing I know he is doing a video blog review of *Keep Swinging* from Helsinki. It was another one of those crazy moments. My book had officially gone global! It truly had taken me and the company to places we never dreamed we could be.

Stepping Up to the Plate

Key ways you can use your book as your hook to grow your business:

1. **Writing a book about your business helps increase customer relations.** When you are asking your customers to spend lots of money with your company, it only makes sense for them to better know who they are dealing with. This is particularly important with remote customers whom you may never meet in person. Sending a copy of my book to all of ISI's clients enhanced our relationship with these clients and gave them a better sense of who we were as a company and who I am as the owner.

2. **A book about your business is the best business card ever.** Business books are typically a means of educating the reader, but for an entrepreneurial author, they can also promote the company. And books are always more impressive than corporate brochures.

3. **Being an author provides a competitive differentiator.** Writing a book creates instant credibility and positions the author as a subject matter expert, which is a very different approach, particularly in my industry. In technology, most of my industry peers write about tech stuff, which is a lot of bits and bytes and frankly not very interesting to read. Writing a book about entrepreneurship and overcoming obstacles in

business and life has a broader, more interesting appeal. And it's different and sets you apart. That's the key.

4. **Being an author gives you an instant marketing and promotional advantage.** Getting a book published opens doors to the media, newspaper, radio, and TV that would be hard to get to otherwise. It also opens up opportunities for public speaking engagements. In the past five years I have given more than fifty speeches to various community groups, including Rotary and Kiwanis, as well as numerous colleges and university classes, as previously noted. Each and every time I speak I do a five-minute overview of ISI, explaining what we do, our products, and our services. It's a priceless opportunity to promote the company in a very focused, professional environment.

CHAPTER 5

TIME TO DOUBLE DOWN

Despite our exhilaration in 2008, it seemed 2009 was going to be a challenge from the get-go. It just didn't seem to be our year. And it wasn't just us. In 2009, reports were telling us that American families were facing the worst economy since the Great Depression. By December 2009, 15.3 million people were unemployed, bringing the unemployment rate to 10.0 percent, twice as many as were unemployed at the start of the recession in December 2007.[10]

The "Great Recession" continued its merciless pace and went even deeper than previously estimated, reflecting slumps in technology spending but even bigger slumps in consumer spending and housing, according to revised figures. The US economy shrank 4.1 percent from the fourth quarter of 2007 to the second quarter of 2009, compared

---

10   Bureau of Labor Statistics, www.bls.gov/data.

with the 3.7 percent drop previously on the books. Normally we don't pay a lot of attention to that kind of news at ISI, but it was getting hard to ignore. To exacerbate the situation even further, all of us had heard the nightly news reports of how household spending fell 1.2 percent in 2009, twice as much as previously projected, which made for the biggest decline in over 67 years.

The slump hit us too, and harder than we ever thought possible. I've got to admit it was tough. Things had been going along so well, and then it just slowed down. People who were crazy busy for so many years were now looking for things to do. Sales contracts we were sure we were going to get either got put on hold or were pushed out much later in the year. Phone calls and emails following up on proposals and deals were running into dead ends. It was scary. I didn't want to lay anybody off, but I also wanted to stay in business and not go bankrupt. "What is the next move?" I was asked many times. "I'll get back to you on that," I responded.

Truth be told, it was hard to figure out how we were going to get things moving again. Hell, the Fortune 500 companies were struggling, so why not ISI as well? It felt like the company was at a crossroads of sorts.

When you're growing a business, a funny thing happens. You get so caught up in the hoopla when it's ramping up that you never consider there are other ways to do business. Onward and upward is always the motto. And as entrepreneurs, we are all paid to essentially do one thing: grow our businesses. When that is not happening, it runs so counter to our DNA that we automatically assume something is terribly wrong. *Yet the ability to navigate a down year may be one of the most important traits that successful entrepreneurs need to develop in order to sustain their business over the long haul.*

As noted earlier, I believe one's character is defined in the moment of crisis. A great example of this was also my favorite moment of 2009 when one of our account managers, Jeremy Johnson, was giving his sales report at the mid-year sales meeting.

Although he was our most experienced rep, he was struggling big-time and seemed to have a run of incredibly bad luck with a number of customers and prospects (due in no small part to the effects of the worldwide recession). And he could have easily buried his head in the sand and had a yearlong pity party. I've seen it time and time again, and it's not a pretty sight.

But successful people can stare down adversity and move on, or try other strategies to disarm a stressful situation. Know what happened in this case? After coming clean about some pretty poor numbers, Jeremy got up and said without hesitation, "I'm off to a rough start. But I know I'm going to do better, because I'm pretty sure my customers can't buy any less than they have so far." At first, I was taken aback. *Are you kidding me?* I was thinking. But you know what? It turned out to be the ultimate icebreaker, and the whole sales team broke out in laughter. Humor is an amazing antidote to even the most stressful of situations. Interestingly enough, a few months after that meeting, Jeremy brought in a contract worth more than $3 million with a major federal government account, which kept ISI profitable in 2009.

I can assure you that everyone at ISI breathed a sigh of relief when that order came in. It was a great comeback for both Jeremy and ISI, for sure—but how do those things happen? Is it luck? Or is there another ingredient? Based on my experience at ISI and other companies, I personally think it all starts and ends with one word and one word only: *attitude*. Whether it's overcoming a slow start in sales or any other issue that has come up over the years, I think the edge that ISI has over other companies is simply our attitude. A positive attitude permeates an organization and serves you well in good and not so good times. I think the positive attitude of the company was a key component of the company's success in 2009, even when we dropped $1 million in sales from the prior year.

As an entrepreneur and a leader, you don't have the luxury to bury your head in the sand just because you had a drop in revenue. Your employees expect you as the leader to show them the way and paint the vision for the future.

Certainly, with the worldwide economic crisis, these are very challenging times to be running a business. People are scared and have lost trust in their leaders. Can you blame them? Remember the stories we heard on almost a daily basis about greedy, dishonest men who deceived their customers and employees in an effort to create ridiculous wealth? Even today, you only have to turn on the TV to hear the latest horror story about Ponzi schemes, deception, and betrayal. This certainly isn't the ideal economic environment to work in, but what can we as leaders and small business owners do to manage our companies in these troubled times? How do you assure your employees, suppliers, and customers? All of these people have a vested interest in your company, so it's best to keep them in the loop.

First, let them know you will take care of them no matter what, and you won't compromise company ethics or integrity to do it. Besides a positive attitude, I can't emphasize enough how important it is to instill confidence in the organization. As we discussed in the last chapter, it's crucial that as the face of the company and the leader you not only have a positive attitude, but also always carry yourself in a confident manner. That in turn instills in others an air of confidence as to where the company is going and how you're going to get there. This is just as true whether you're facing a temporary downward trend in your company's numbers or facing a major longer-lasting industry or worldwide economic downturn.

After all, your employees are getting their cues from you. If you panic, they panic. It's hard to not show concern in these difficult times, but it should not be normal demeanor for an effective leader. Think about it from your employees' perspective. If you're calm, they're calm. If you get rattled, they get rattled.

It's amazing to me that many small business owners (and Fortune 500 CEOs) still struggle on a daily basis with this very basic leadership concept. How do you expect your employees to perform and move forward when they get something less than confidence from their leader? It's all in how you present yourself.

All of this reminds me of a concept I heard about many years ago when I first started my career in sales: the self-fulfilling prophesy. If you dwell on a negative outcome, that's what you tend to get. But it works both ways: In order to be successful at doing something, you need to close your eyes and picture yourself delivering the most successful outcome prior to actually doing it. Picture yourself closing a successful sale or giving a successful speech. Whatever you need to do, go through all the motions as you imagine it happening as vividly as possible. It's like a mental dress rehearsal, and it works.

Many professional athletes have done this for years. I've been told that Jack Nicklaus used this strategy many times in his long, successful career in professional golf, which included winning eighteen major championships. Nicklaus would picture the crucial putt going in way before it actually happened. This kind of mental discipline works in most any profession. Small business owners who lead with confidence and a positive mindset use the strategy of self-fulfilling prophesy to communicate success to their employees and are generally the ones that come out on top.

Once we got our attitude straight, it hit me. Maybe deciding our next move didn't have to be that complicated. Maybe the answer to a down year was to just keep doing what we're good at, just like it was after we lost so many key people. ISI had been successful in several niche markets like distance learning and telemedicine for a number of years, so why not simply refocus our efforts to support those opportunities? Rather than trying to get into new products or markets that we had little or no experience in, didn't it make more sense to do like the gamblers do at the casinos and double down?

In particular, we decided to focus on niche marketing with our rural health care and telemedicine products and services. What is telemedicine, you might ask? Telemedicine (also referred to as telehealth or e-health) allows health care professionals to evaluate, diagnose, and treat patients in remote locations using telecommunications technology. Telemedicine has become standard medical practice and is in daily use across dozens of countries. More than 10,000 peer-reviewed papers have been published over the past twenty years supporting the clinical effectiveness and cost savings of telemedicine.

Telemedicine not only allows clinicians to "see" patients in multiple locations wherever they are needed without leaving their facility, but it also allows local practitioners to consult with their peers and with clinical experts when needed, alleviating the sense of isolation clinicians in remote areas often experience. And it also allows them to participate in grand rounds and education opportunities they would not normally have access to without travel and time away from their patients.

The need for rural health care in ISI's six-state area of Tennessee, Arkansas, Mississippi, Louisiana, Alabama and Kentucky is profound. For some rural areas where people must drive 200 miles to see a specialist, telemedicine will allow more people to be seen more quickly by the right doctor for their need. Unfortunately, most rural community hospitals do not have basic patient-assessment capability in place on an around-the-clock basis. Put simply, telemedicine can provide the right care faster, save lives when minutes count, and allow rural hospitals to compete in the twenty-first century and offer rural citizens access to the same quality medical care that urban citizens enjoy.

Besides providing a big feel-good opportunity to ISI about what we are doing with technology to improve people's lives, there was a practical business side as to why it made sense to double down on our investment in telemedicine. Two words: It's hot. Since ISI installed our first telemedicine system in 1998, revenues have increased from $50,000 to more than $12 million in 2011, and we're projecting even more in the years ahead.

Man of the Hour. *It was a fun night getting a chance to recognize Michael Sanders (right) for winning the largest contract in ISI history at UAMS for $8.3 million in telemedicine equipment.*

After all, we have learned a lot about the technology since those early days. The awkward, clunky carts we sold in 1998 utilized a few very expensive peripheral scopes and tools. We have since refined our offering to a sleek, customized unit that can easily be accessed to support cardiology, dermatology, psychiatry, and other advanced applications at a very high level. We have even integrated a combination scope into our system where we can support high-quality ear, nose, and throat examinations with the same device, swapping out couplers, covers, and more.

We can't help but be proud of the part we're playing in improving and even saving lives. In fact, our technology literally helped save the life of a gunshot victim in Mississippi by instantly connecting the small community hospital (a Level 3 trauma center) to the Level 1 trauma center in Jackson. Basic triage was performed at the rural hospital via the tele-emergency connection, and the specialists and surgeons in Jackson were able to coach doctors and nurse practicioners through various procedures to buy enough time to transport the patient to Jackson for emergency surgery. According to hospital officials, had that not happened, the patient would have died.

Also, several months ago, we installed a number of telemedicine carts for a network in Arkansas specifically set up to treat stroke victims. If you look at a map showing the incidence of stroke across the United States, you'll see a surprisingly dense cluster in one particular area, the southeastern United States. Americans living in this region have a 15 percent higher stroke risk, and the death rate from stroke in these "stroke belt" states is 30 to 40 percent higher than in the rest of the country. Since stroke patients typically require specialized treatment, it is even more difficult to get this level of support from a small rural hospital.

That was the dilemma facing one patient recently when he experienced stroke-like symptoms and needed help. At the time, driving several hours to Little Rock to see a specialist was not an option. There was simply not enough time. With time being of the essence, the patient was quickly transported to the local hospital and got immediate help from a nurse practicioner and a specialist via our telestroke connection. The patient, who had a life-threatening condition one day, was back at work two days later. All of this was possible because of the immediate support provided by the telestroke network. It doesn't get any better than that for a business!

In addition to telemedicine, ISI also redoubled its efforts in the area of distance learning. In the past decade, distance education has become an increasingly popular way for colleges to provide access to their programs and for students to learn about topics and get degrees they might not otherwise be able to pursue.

Instructors from grade school to college are using the potential of distance learning to teach students from all around the globe and allow them to work collaboratively on projects, degree-focused content, and educational enrichment.

Throughout the states of Tennessee, Mississippi, and Alabama, ISI has installed hundreds of distance learning labs and classrooms that allow students to attend classes with specialized content from hundreds of miles away. Similar to the issues in health care, there is a profound shortage of teachers and instructors to teach specialized courses in engineering, calculus, German, French, and so on in rural areas. Many colleges and universities have faced losing their accreditation if they didn't solve the problem of providing support to students in rural communities.

Maybe that's the key to niche marketing that is so important, particularly with technology. Any technology product, no matter how cool it is, is worthless if it doesn't solve a business problem, pure and simple. ISI's telemedicine systems are doing great things for the community, but they are also solving a business problem.

That problem is that rural communities require a higher level of specialized support, and the hospital needs to be able to fulfill it— and do so profitably. In other words, the technology might work just fine, but the key to profitability is the fact that the hospital can get reimbursed by Medicare and Medicaid for the visits, just as if the doctor were there in person. In that way, patients get high-level medical support and the hospitals make money, which translates to the best of both worlds.

The same strategy applies with the colleges and universities, where the students are charged a technology access fee as part of providing support of distance learning classrooms throughout the various states. The students get a chance to take a class remotely in their local community that many times they need in order to graduate. In turn, the school charges for tuition the same way it does for any other class. That's a winning combination.

So in 2009, we used all of these strategies and more to deal with the downturn in the economy when it showed up in our numbers. We maintained a positive attitude despite the economic challenges, carried ourselves confidently, pictured ourselves being profitable and successful, and got back to the basics with niche marketing and redoubling our efforts to do what we did best. In the end, not only did we navigate a tough year, but we also used it as motivation to do even better in 2010 and set the company on a trajectory for growth like we had never seen before.

Stepping Up **to the Plate**

Key ways a company can use a down year to sharpen its mindset:

1. **Maintain a positive attitude every day.** It is important for your company to see that you as their leader have a firm hand on the wheel and will guide the company to a successful future.

2. **Instill confidence in your employees.** A confident leader is an effective one, so make sure that your employees see that in you. Nervous, uncertain leaders make for skittish employees and less than successful companies.

3. **Maintain your sense of humor.** Running a company isn't curing cancer. It's a business. It's important to earn revenue and profit, but it's important to keep it in perspective. Lighten up!

4. **Envision a successful self-fulfilling prophesy.** Picture yourself being successful, and teach your employees to do the same.

5. **Get back to the basics with niche marketing.** Don't reinvent the wheel in a down year, and don't try to be all things to all people. Identify one or two of your company's most profitable niches, and make your niche your brand. Develop a game plan to be the very best at one or two things and work continually on those products and services. Evaluate what it will take to sell more to those areas, and build a business model that can scale to that level.

CHAPTER 6

CREATING A LEGACY

. . . [I]n the end, being an entrepreneur is more than ever the way you can choose your path and find the deep satisfaction of walking it. You can earn your days without being beholden. You can make something affect the world, leave something behind where once nothing stood. You can turn work into meaning for yourself and for others. You can be proud. You can leave a wake. Come good or ill, you can assume responsibility for yourself, and be whole, and be who you were meant to be.[11]

I read a lot of articles and quotes in *Inc.* magazine, but this is by far my favorite one. It sums up perfectly why I do what I do at ISI. You see, it's never been about the money with me—it never has been and

---

11   Michael Hopkins, "75 Reasons to Be Glad You're an American Entrepreneur Right Now," *Inc.*, October 1, 2005.

never will be. Now I would be lying if I said the money I've earned at ISI hasn't been really good, because it certainly has been. But building a successful business has a lot more meaning for me than just how much money I can put in my bank account.

To be sure, we have been fortunate at ISI to have grown the business at a nice clip for almost seventeen years now and maintained profitability. And our success has been good enough to have earned significant recognition for our efforts, like making the Inc. 500/5000 list of fastest-growing private companies in the United States seven times since 2001. All of us are not only proud of what we've done to grow ISI, but we've done so in the crazy world of high tech and amid the challenges of the relentless worldwide economic downturn.

But for me that is simply not enough. I don't want ISI to just be successful; I want it to be significant as well. At the end of the day, I want to use ISI as a platform to make a difference not only in my local community, but also beyond.

And how did I come up with this profound strategy? It probably stems from one word that I return to over and over again in my career as an entrepreneur. It's a word I think about on a daily basis as CEO of ISI. That word is "gratitude." What is gratitude? The *World English Dictionary* defines it as "a feeling of thankfulness or appreciation," which is certainly the way that I feel about the success of ISI seventeen years later.

It has certainly been a difficult path to get to where we are today, and maybe that's why I feel so grateful. In this life, how many people can truly say that they are living their dream? It sounds corny, I know, but it is also true. I'm the guy who made Cs in school, and now I'm running a $25 million technology business. And I'm not even technical! Ask my wife. I'm the guy who had the zeroes blinking on his VCR for months before I figured out how to set the clock.

But somehow I found this little niche called video conferencing way back in 1990 and have been able to make a really good living at it for a long time. Yes, we have had to overcome a lot of obstacles through the years, including getting fired, surviving cancer (both me and my wife), a partnership divorce, employee embezzlement, employee turnover, and a host of financial issues. It certainly hasn't been a walk in the park, but with God's help, the company and I are still around, doing our best to keep the ball rolling and provide a living for my fifty-plus employees.

ISI has come a long way. But how does a successful long-term business give back? How do we show the gratitude that I personally feel is so important? For years, one way has been through the ISI Gives Back program, which allows our employees to request funds for a charity of their choice, whether it be a church, school, or community organization. ISI Gives Back was the brainchild of my wife, Maureen, after we survived the embezzlement of 2003, and it has worked out very well. It has gotten our employees fully engaged in thinking about community service. Here's how it works. The ISI employee identifies a charitable opportunity to donate either time or money to (or both) and sends in a formal written request for approval (and most are approved).

The company likes to do things on a continual basis if possible and supports efforts like the Morgan McCarty Fund (www. morganmemsch.com) which honors the memory of a young college student at the University of Tennessee who was killed several years ago by a hit and run driver as she was walking home. Other ISI Gives Back initiatives include donations to St. Patrick's Catholic Church in downtown Memphis. St. Patrick's is a unique place in many ways, especially when you consider its location. It is situated a few hundred feet across the street from one of the premier sports venues in the country, the FedExForum, a $300 million state-of-the-art sports and entertainment complex that holds more than 19,000 people.

Tale of Two Cities. *St. Patrick's Church (left) is located just a few hundred feet from the FedExForum.*

Yet the demographics of St. Patrick's congregation represent the third-poorest zip code in the United States. It was unbelievable to think that people are spending more money on a basketball season ticket than many of the people across the street make in an entire year. That doesn't seem right. So ISI wanted to step in and support St. Patrick's by donating and installing several pieces of technology equipment for the church's learning center. Being a Memphis-based company, we are proud that Memphis has been rated the number two most charitable community in the country.[12] As a caring community, it's in the DNA of Memphis to give back, and it happens all day, every day, by many groups all across our community. That's why I see our ISI Gives Back program as an obligation, not an option. Also, as the owner of ISI, I particularly like the fact that I don't make all the decisions about how we

12   Ben Gose, "How America Gives," *Chronicle of Philanthropy,* August 19, 2012, www. philanthropy.com.

Creating a Legacy Takes Teamwork. *Maureen and I are both committed to ISI not just being a successful company but a significant one as well.*

distribute the company's charitable donations. It's a total team effort, not the Jay and Maureen show all the time.

But what else can companies do besides write a check in order to create a lasting legacy for the company? My personal belief is that you have to invest not only your money, but your time as well. Writing checks is easy, but giving your time means so much more.

ISI didn't get to where we are today without the help of many people along the way who advised or acted as a mentor to me and the company. As I reflect on my career as an entrepreneur, I must say I have had a lot of good mentors in the early days of ISI, and I think it is so important in the development of any business. Sometimes you just need someone you can call to get an experienced, unbiased view of whatever problem or issue has been presented, someone who has walked through the fire. Or in some cases, the mentor provides a learning environment where knowledge is being developed on a daily or weekly basis.

One such program that I have been involved with in the Memphis area has been the Seed Hatchery, a mentorship-driven seed-stage investment program. Seed Hatchery supports emerging technology entrepreneurs with capital and strategic mentors to sharpen ideas into strong start-ups in exchange for a small stake in the business. The really cool thing about the Seed Hatchery program is that there is a finite time to get the business off the ground, which is typically ninety days, and each program cohort includes three to six start-ups. In the ninety-day program, each company is provided business advice and technical assistance to refine the product or service, strengthen the business model, form the operations, begin marketing efforts, and determine the market viability of the business.

My involvement with Seed Hatchery has been as a mentor assisting several start-up firms, like StiQRd, which is a loyalty and rewards smartphone app and platform. Customers are using the free StiQRd app to find participating retailers, snap QR codes, and claim rewards and discounts. Business owners can use StiQRd to create and manage promotions to reward repeat customers. When I first heard about StiQRd, I thought it was a cool idea that made a lot of sense. I also saw that the company founders were really good, hardworking guys with lots of passion who were risking everything to get their business off the ground. I thought, *These are my kind of people,* so when it came time to offer mentor assistance, I gladly offered to help them out.

There have been other companies, like Smarter City, that envision connecting the physical world to the Internet via a citywide sensor network. In this way, day-to-day challenges like finding downtown parking can be automated to the point of identifying unoccupied parking spaces in advance. Garage owners can receive valuable information on usage that saves them money and also makes for a happier satisfied customer. Pie in the sky? Maybe so, but there's a side of me that vividly remembers back in 1996 when every banker in town thought I had lost my mind trying to start a video conferencing company. "What exactly is that stuff?" I was asked. "Sounds like George Jetson," another banker responded. Suffice it to say, none of them thought it was a good idea to invest in a business that they didn't understand or think had a future. So I guess that's exactly why I wanted to help out the Seed Hatchery folks. It's easy to invest in a sure thing, but not one in its early stages and so uncertain.

There are other ways to give back to the community through mentorship. For example, ISI recently became involved with the Memphis Catholic High School Education That Works (ETW) program. The focus of the ETW program is urban education, and its purpose is to equip financially less fortunate students to ultimately complete college and launch a successful career. The ETW student body resembles the racial makeup of the city of Memphis, with 75 percent black, 4 percent Hispanic, 3 percent African, 2 percent Asian, 9 percent white, and 7 percent multiracial students. These same students come from thirty zip codes in the metropolitan area; 75 percent are non-Catholics, and 25 percent are Catholics.

ETW is designed to provide students with few financial options a high-quality private college preparatory education. More than half of the ETW families qualify for federal free or reduced lunch programs and more than 60 percent of the students receive donor-funded financial assistance with their ETW tuition. In addition, each student earns two-thirds of their tuition by working five full days every month for an ETW sponsor firm; ISI has been one of those companies since August 2011.

The really special part of this program for us is that it is so much more than writing a check. When our ETW student would get off the bus and enter our office, it was like he was entering a whole new world. We didn't want our ETW student just doing busy work; we wanted to show him what it's like to be a part of a successful business that was built out of dirt.

This proved to be an invaluable experience for our ETW student. For example, our 2012–2013 student got a chance to do so many things in the year he was at our office. Whether he was working in our build room assembling medical carts for our telemedicine projects or converting our old paper files to digital (by scanning them) we tried to show him the many facets of our business, and he liked it. It truly is a win-win proposition, because all of us enjoyed helping prepare this young man for the future. Hopefully, as he looks back on his high school days, he will remember a few things we tried to teach him about working hard, presenting a professional image, and good old-fashioned teamwork. In the end, that's not a bad legacy to pass on to the next generation. But there are other ways to give back, which we discovered in the spring of 2011—courtesy of Mother Nature.

From April 25 to 28, 2011, the largest single-system tornado outbreak ever recorded in the United States cut a swath across Arkansas, Georgia, Mississippi, Tennessee, Virginia, and Alabama. In total, 348 people were killed as a result of the outbreak. Alabama was the hardest hit state, and on April 27, Tuscaloosa was in the bull's-eye of the storm.

More than 5,000 homes in the city alone were damaged or destroyed and hundreds of businesses were affected in the area, according to the West Alabama Chamber of Commerce. The storm cut a six-mile-long path through the city, destroying or damaging about 12 percent of it, according to Tuscaloosa officials. The tornado left enough debris to fill Bryant-Denny Stadium five times, Mayor Walt Maddox said.

The Tuscaloosa tornado was given a rating of EF4, which is the second most powerful tornado on the Enhanced Fujita scale. This means it had sustained wind speeds between 166 and 200 mph. The storm claimed fifty-three lives in Tuscaloosa that fateful day.

Like everyone else in the country, all of us at ISI watched in horror as images from the deadly tornadoes flashed on our TVs night after night. With the mounting death toll, it was hard to watch. Tuscaloosa is located in central Alabama, a little less than three hours from Memphis and even a little closer to our office in Nashville. It is, of course, home to the University of Alabama, who has been a loyal ISI client for more than ten years. In that time, ISI has installed equipment in various distance learning and smart classrooms throughout the campus with great success and has built a strong client-vendor relationship.

In addition to the strong business relationship, ISI has also enjoyed a close personal relationship with many of the university employees and staff who support our equipment. Many individuals are more than just customers; they're our friends. So when the tornado hit Tuscaloosa that tragic afternoon last April, it felt like it hit us, too. And it hurt—a lot. Our friends had been dealt a tragic blow and they needed help. Night after night we viewed the devastation on TV. It was hard to watch.

Path of Destruction. *The Tuscaloosa tornadoes appeared in a few minutes and changed lives forever.*

A few days after the storm, we tried to call to get a status report on them and the rest of Tuscaloosa. No response. On the next day there was still no response. We were getting more concerned by the minute. Hours seemed like days and days seemed like weeks. It was scary.

And then finally we got the word: everyone was alive and well. Thank God. We all breathed a sigh of relief. Of course, they still had a rough time ahead, with half their town destroyed. These folks had been through a living hell that most people never see in a lifetime. It was gut-wrenching.

Several weeks after the storm, after the TV cameras had moved on from the Tuscaloosa tornado story and with the images from the storm fresh on my mind, I decided to call a meeting at ISI. I posed a simple question: "What can we do to help our friends in Tuscaloosa?"

At first there was silence, and then someone spoke up. "Not sure what we can do, but we need to do something," one employee replied. "But what?"

My accounts receivable manager, Linda Mathis, offered a suggestion. "Why don't I call down there and see what they need?" she asked.

"Great idea," I replied.

"We could send them a check," one employee suggested.

"Not this time," I replied. "This is too close to home. I want to do more—these are our friends we're talking about."

Linda called and inquired about the Tuscaloosa Disaster Relief Fund, which had recently been set up to assist victims of the storm. She touched base with various groups in Tuscaloosa to get a list of specific items that people there needed, such as canned food, clothing, toiletries, and so on. One of the biggest needs that we discovered was dog food! We found out that people weren't the only ones hurting after the storm. For days, Linda and several employees went about the task of securing items needed to assist the Tornado Relief Fund.

It was so gratifying to see ISI employees stepping out of their weekly office routine and pulling together for a good cause—a cause that meant something to us, because it was personal. And maybe because it was personal, it somehow didn't seem enough to just pack up all the items and ship them down to Tuscaloosa. That seemed too easy, and it just didn't feel right. "These people are our friends," I told our employees again. "Let's go down to Tuscaloosa and personally deliver everything. Let's not just tell them we care—let's show them."

Why did I choose to do that? We could have easily shipped everything down there, kept everybody at the office working, and felt good about making a charitable donation. Everybody would go home feeling good about themselves and call it a day. But I made that decision for a reason. I didn't want us to go there to take credit for what we were doing and pat ourselves on the back. That wasn't our style. No, it was to see firsthand what total devastation looks like, which was an experience none of us in Memphis had ever had to deal with. You can't fake that kind of stuff.

I wanted them to see what it looks like when people lose everything: their homes, their businesses, and their community. I also wanted them to see what effect the storm had on our customers down there, people we knew. We didn't go down there as some sort of heroic gesture, but to demonstrate that ISI truly cares about our customers— not just for the money they spend with us, but for the people they are. Talk is cheap. Actions speak louder than words. First and foremost, these are human beings we're talking about, who are also our friends, and they were hurting.

I remember making the three-hour drive from Memphis that day, thinking about how tough it was going to be for these people to have to go through the long process of rebuilding their community and their lives. Everything changed in a minute. They had a house, and then they didn't. It was tragic. Rebuilding certainly wouldn't be done overnight.

When we arrived in Tuscaloosa, I remember my first reaction. It was a gasp of horror. Crumbled brick and concrete were all that was left where homes and businesses once stood. It was a sickening feeling. Everywhere we looked there was devastation: collapsed buildings, roofs blown off, restaurants and small businesses leveled. As far as the eye could see there were piles and piles of rubble. Based on what we saw that day, I was wondering how anybody in Tuscaloosa made it out alive.

Tuscaloosa Disaster. *Whole series of buildings destroyed after the tornadoes of 2011.*

When we finally located the drop-off center, I remember the volunteers motioning to where they wanted us to place the various food and clothing items we had brought. It was a huge warehouse, and as we started to unload the truck and walk in, I stared in amazement at the amount of donations they had already collected. Food, clothing, and household items were stacked from the floor to the ceiling, row after row. It was amazing to see the generosity of people in such a short time. It also warmed my heart that people still cared these days.

For the ISI group that made the trip, we all felt good that, in a very small way, we were doing our part to help out a community in need. On our way out of town I remember seeing a sign on top of a pile of rubble that was once a fast-food restaurant. It had a tattered American flag attached to it, and it simply said, WE WILL COME BACK. I had a lump in my throat. Amid all this death and destruction, the character, guts, and determination of these people was beyond remarkable. I for one left town that day knowing that even though it would take a long time to rebuild their town, the citizens of Tuscaloosa would indeed come back.

Stepping Up to the Plate

Key ways you can create a legacy with your business:

1. **Examine your beliefs and your passions.** Identify a cause you can get behind that truly means something to you and the business. Don't do it only because it looks good on your resume.

2. **Get involved.** Become a mentor; help others through actions. Giving money is easy. Giving your time takes effort. Also, mentoring young people can have lifelong benefits, for you and for them.

3. **Get your hands dirty.** Don't take the easy way out. Whether it's driving a few hours one day to deliver food and clothing to storm victims or helping out others less fortunate, get out of your office and make a difference. Whether it's for one day, one month, or one year, get out of your comfort zone and think about somebody besides yourself and your company for a change.

CHAPTER 7

PLATEAU OR GROW?

One of the most difficult issues that small business owners face after they have been in business for a number of years can be summed up in one word: complacency. What exactly do I mean by that? Complacency is the natural tendency to think that since the business has been around five, ten, or fifteen years, it will go along forever. This is especially true if the business has built up a book of business and repeat customers make up a majority of the annual revenue year in and year out.

Certainly as a small business owner it is critical to have repeat customers, and hopefully customers for life, if at all possible. But how does a business keep growing these days? What is it about some companies that have the "it" factor, while others are satisfied with just barely getting by? Based on my experience, it all starts with your people. A growing business has to have the right people in place to be able to navigate the many challenges of getting a business off the ground and subsequently move to the next level.

This is where it gets increasingly difficult: Entrepreneurs must assemble the right team to get the job done year in and year out. As painful as it is, many times the people you hire in the start-up phase are not going to be the people who take you to the next level. Why is that? Why can't they make the transition? One reason is that people who enjoy the start-up environment are just a little different. This doesn't make them bad or good, just different. Most are hardworking, risk-taking adrenaline junkies who enjoy the informal, unstructured style of a start-up environment. There's nothing wrong with any of that, but over time they can become disconnected with a growing company with its eye on the future.

When you continue to employ the wrong people for the wrong reasons, these same people can kill your company and destroy your dreams. It's just that simple. Yet it's also complex. How do you know when to make changes in your personnel to keep your organization growing? What warning signs do you need to look for?

Let's take the first question, which is deciding when you need to make changes in your organization. Based on my experience with ISI, the first place you want to look is with your customers. Does this individual deal well with your customers? Are you getting any complaints about him or the quality of his work? Since customers pay the bills at ISI, they are our number one priority, so how an employee deals with clients is critical.

Suppliers may also be key to the company's success. For instance, suppliers are an important component of a value-added reseller (VAR) company like ISI, and many times our relationships with suppliers can make the difference between success and failure. If there is no direct customer or supplier contact to evaluate, then the employee may need to be evaluated based on internal feedback as well. Is this employee a team player? Are they getting the job done internally?

Whether or not the employee is tenured, you need to pose these questions regularly to make sure you have the right employee on board, regardless of the amount of time he has worked for you. What does Jim Collins say in his book *Good to Great* (HarperCollins, 2001)? You have to have the right people on the bus in order to grow a profitable company. Sometimes employees start out on the bus and do exactly what the company needs—and then years later have a hard time keeping up the skill set to stay on the bus. Simply put, the skill set required to get a company off the ground is not the same as the one that will maintain and grow a $5 million, $10 million, or $50 million company.

What's the difference? Many times it involves basic leadership skills. As a company grows, you have to build a management team that can recruit and build a team as well as effectively delegate. Growing a larger organization involves more meetings and more organization, and less flying by the seat of your pants. Many people in start-up environments thrive on the chaotic, informal environment and actually get a thrill out of the uncertainty. Most of them hate meetings of any kind.

But as a business owner trying to grow your business, you can do that for only so long. Soon it's time to grow up. And just like it is with people, growing up can be an awkward, sometimes painful process.

I must say, as the founder and owner of ISI, I have always had a soft spot in my heart for the people who helped me get started and who helped build my business. But how do you know when it's time to grow up? Are there warning signs associated with a tenured employee who needs to go? Are there things that you can pick up on to help make your decision? Sure there are.

The first one is a no-brainer: you cannot and should not ever be spending a significant amount of your time arguing or disagreeing with an employee, no matter what the issue is. There is nothing wrong with healthy debate between people here and there, but it cannot be constant. It can eat up an enormous amount of time. I know this for a fact, because it happened at ISI.

As the leader of the company, you need to make sure your other employees aren't distracted by this behavior. Employees who fight with the company owner are usually fighting with other people in the company as well. When that happens, overall company productivity goes down, and the instigating employee needs to go. With the many other challenges facing companies these days, the last thing an owner needs to do is waste time with a problem child in the organization.

Additional warning signs can be a little less obvious. Constantly talking about the good old days or not embracing changes or new procedures can also be a tip-off. A typical start-up business experiencing fast growth looks very different after three, four, and five years than it did on day one. It looks even more different ten, twelve, and fifteen years later. And sometimes it's a look some people simply don't like or want to be a part of. The sad truth is that when a company grows, some employees either can't step up their game or choose not to do so.

Businesses have to evolve to survive in today's competitive world, and so do employees. Through the years, ISI has had employee issues like every business. We've hired people who get it, who've been with the company for many years and done well, and we've hired some who never did get it and had to go at one point or another. But how do you know for sure when an employee needs to go?

I once heard a nationally recognized radio host state that "as the business owner, if you go home at night and complain about an employee more than three times, they need to go." But what if the employee has been with you five, ten, or more years? Should you have a different strategy for those folks? Are businesses like colleges or universities? Do employees have tenure? This last one's easy: No! Not unless your business is a nonprofit, like a school.

The key to making good personnel decisions, tenured or not, is to first determine the real value of the employee *today*. That doesn't mean six months or six years ago, but *today*. Because businesses have to make a profit to survive, this means you must continually evaluate your people and your processes. No matter how hard it is, small business owners have to decide what is best for the business as a whole. In order for a business to grow, it needs occasional pruning in order for the growth process to continue. We did just that at ISI in 2012, and it was painful and personal. But in order to move forward, you have to be able to make tough decisions and put together the best team possible.

What else does a business need to grow, besides getting your people right? Another important key is to make sure you have adequate structures and financing in place to support the growth. If you don't do this right, you can literally "grow broke." Sound absurd? It's not.

I've heard countless stories of fast-growth companies that have experienced meteoric increases in revenue in short periods of time, only to find out that their companies aren't set up to support the growth. I experienced that firsthand, having attended a number of the Inc. 500 conferences across the country for a number of years. *Inc.* magazine, of course, is the bible for small business owners and annually publishes its Inc. 5000 list of fastest-growing private companies in the United States. Being named to the list is quite an honor and carries a lot of prestige. Of course, being named number one on the list is a huge accomplishment.

But ironically enough, I recently read that the number one company on the Inc. list a few years back is now scrambling to stay in business. Talk about one and done! Unfortunately it's all too common when a company is not set up to support rapid growth; the wheels can and will come off at some point. As good as it might appear on the surface, dramatic increases in revenue for any company can create serious growing pains that must be dealt with.

To get your company structurally and financially ready to support rapid growth, you need to pay attention to at least three basic issues:

1. **Staffing requirements.** Does your business have enough qualified personnel to get the job done, both now and in the foreseeable future? A business owner really needs to spend time thoroughly understanding the company's labor needs, because without good people, the company will not grow.

2. **Tight controls on accounts receivable** to ensure adequate cash flow to meet obligations. That means that the vast majority (more than 90 percent) of your customers need to pay you within terms (thirty days or less) to assist in funding your company's growth. At ISI, we have an obsession with accounts receivable and cash flow.

I learned a long time ago that cash is king for a small, growing company. If you're not on top of it every day, you can go out of business very quickly. That's why accounts receivable issues are a key topic at my management team meetings every Friday morning. If we have a problem with an account not paying us, we discuss it as a team and make sure we have all our bases covered before we make the next move. And we are aggressive about our collection process. Our accounts receivable manager has a single focus in her ISI job description, which is to make sure clients pay us within terms and to have as few as possible (if any) aging receivables of more than thirty days in her weekly report.

Another related, successful portion of ISI's overall accounts receivable strategy has been the simple matter of requesting down payments from customers. Getting money down on a large contract can make all the difference in the world in establishing a smooth transaction (with equipment deliveries, for example) and a successfully implemented project. In this way, ISI partners with our clients in order to achieve a win-win for both organizations and subsequently be able to position ourselves for an increase in sales revenue.

This strategy worked very well recently when ISI won a major contract in Arkansas worth more than $8 million. By working hand in hand with the customer, not only did we work out reasonable payment terms, but we met our supplier and ISI banking obligations as well. Everybody won! What was the secret formula? We made sure there was 100 percent transparent communication between all delivery parties, from suppliers to equipment installers to trainers. All expectations from all parties were met: the customer's, ISI's, and the suppliers'. Win-win-win. That's a template that can be used for growth now and in the future.

3. **Access to adequate capital or a line of credit** to be able to navigate the various day-to-day vendor commitments and accommodate business growth. Ever since I got out of college, I have tried my best to avoid using credit of any type, especially credit cards. *Why is that?* you might ask. Doesn't everybody use credit cards? Like, every day?

I guess it goes back to when I was first out of college and got my hands on my first credit card—a nice, shiny MasterCard, mailed to my apartment. Man, did I feel like a big shot! I could go out and buy whatever I wanted by just flashing that card and signing a receipt. And boy, was that fun. My new apartment got furnished quickly. Why wait? If I needed or wanted something, I had my handy dandy MasterCard to make it happen. Need a new lamp? Not a problem. New stereo? Ditto. It was instant gratification, and I had an apartment full of furniture and stuff to show for it. I was truly living the life at the ripe old age of twenty-two.

Then one day the mail came. I thumbed through the various letters and bills, and came across the bill from MasterCard. When

I first read it, I thought it was a misprint and about dropped my teeth. I remember literally shrieking at the time. Surely this was a mistake. How can I have spent $3,000 in one month? Of course, it didn't stop there. The interest rate on this card was more than 18 percent, and I could barely afford the minimum payment. I started to get a sick feeling in my stomach. *This is not good,* I thought. *I've got to do something about it and soon.*

Well, I did take care of my bill, but it took me over a year to get it cleared up. I paid off that $3,000 and did something that I am proud of to this day. I wrote a letter to the president of MasterCard. In it, I told him how much I appreciated the opportunity to use his company's card but that clearly I wasn't mature enough to use it properly and enclosed he would find a check for the balance due as well as the card (cut up in pieces). I told him I would notify him if I ever had interest in getting another MasterCard in the future. That was 1980, and I've never had another interest-bearing credit card since.

So, to say I'm fiscally conservative all these years later may be a significant understatement, but it has served both me and the company well through the years. When we sat down at the 2011 ISI Kickoff Meeting and were looking at a forecast that would grow the company's revenue from $17.5 million to $25 million, with the biggest portion of the growth coming from one very large contract in Arkansas, I knew we needed to make structural changes to accommodate this growth before it happened. Growth is great, but scary, too. It could leave us vulnerable from a financing standpoint. I had already heard about companies growing broke. Of course, not many people would turn down that kind of growth if they had the chance to do it. But still, we were concerned about how we were going to be able to handle everything financially, as well as securing the manpower to complete the project.

I could have just played the dictator, took control, and told everyone what structural changes we were going to implement. But I didn't want my ultraconservative viewpoint to provide the only input on this issue. How ISI handled growth would affect a lot of people in the company, not just me. Instead, I decided to educate my management team about fast growth in a business. They needed the good, the bad, and the ugly parts of the story.

I decided to enlist the help of Doug Tatum, one of my Inc. 500 associates, whom I had heard at a conference several years before. His book *No Man's Land* (Portfolio, 2007) describes companies just like ISI, which "are too big to be small, but too small to be big."

In Doug's book he identifies the four distinct managerial areas (the four Ms) that create difficulty for fast growth companies like ISI. Those four points include:

- A company has to understand the transition in the business's *market*.
- A company has to address the changes that will be required in *management*.
- A company will need to test its economic model to ensure continued profitability as the business scales upward.
- A business needs to understand the practical requirements for attracting the needed *money*.

I bought copies of *No Man's Land* for the entire management team, and reading Doug's book gave us all a lot to think about. Getting into no-man's-land might have been an inevitability, but we sure didn't want to stay there! An added benefit of reading the book together was that every member of the ISI management team got a keener understanding of what their department needed to do for the company to continue to grow and make it out of no-man's-land.

One insight we gained from the book that is a common problem with fast-growth companies like ISI is fulfilling customer promises like a second-grade soccer team: everybody runs instinctively to the ball. All of us understood that to realign with customers and get through no-man's-land, we would need to create a system in which everybody behaves rationally and plays a specific position. It made a lot of sense. Another insight we gained from reading Doug's book was learning the true capital cost of each employee and that it was a lot more than we all previously thought when benefits and overhead were factored in. All things that have to be considered and critical to guide a company through no-man's-land.

Reading a book together as a management team wasn't exactly revolutionary thinking, but as ISI's owner, I'm convinced that getting buy-in from the team regarding the upcoming operational changes was a key ingredient to our success in 2011. What exactly did they buy in to? First off, the message was sent loud and clear that we were all in it together and we had to get better as a team focusing on the four Ms. ISI had operated for many years like the second-grade soccer team, and that wasn't going to cut it anymore. ISI needed more structure for specific positions. The management team also understood we would have to look at shaking up the organization's decision makers and develop more radical thinking to continue to grow in the future. All of them understood that what got ISI here won't keep us here and that we had to grow up to be successful in the future. They also bought in on the fact that if ISI didn't successfully navigate no-man's-land, we were all in trouble.

The decision to educate and solicit input from my management team goes back to my operating philosophy of using as many resources as I can to contribute to the success of the company. Why have a management team if you don't use them to help manage your company? Also, when you invest in educating your team members, they appreciate the respect and the trust you're demonstrating to them. As simple as it sounds, everyone appreciates it when you think enough of them to solicit their opinion and show them that it matters. But maybe even more important was the fact that as the owner, I was communicating that we were all in this together. We were going to make it through no-man's-land as a team, pure and simple.

The final way ISI planned for growth was to make a point of forging an even closer relationship with a key part of our team: our bank. For some business owners, this may sound like heresy, but we've partnered with our bank, BancorpSouth, for years. BancorpSouth is one of the largest banks in the state of Mississippi and has been an ISI client since 1998.

The partnership has worked well, maybe because it reflects their basic operating philosophy, which appears on their website: "For more than 135 years, BancorpSouth has met the banking needs of the communities it serves through a series of community banks managed with an entrepreneurial spirit. Our banks team with their communities to grow by actively participating in public-private partnerships that build communities and provide a better way of life for all of their citizens."

Maybe it's the entrepreneurial spirit ISI and BancorpSouth share that has made our long-term relationship a winning combination. Maybe it's BancorpSouth's intentional partnering philosophy. Or maybe it's both. Whatever it is, it works. And it has for a long time.

Truthfully, today there are a lot of banks who want to do business with us, but we remain loyal to BancorpSouth for a lot of reasons. One is that they continue to be a good ISI customer with our video conferencing and audiovisual equipment, which is consistent with our philosophy of doing business with people who do business with us. Also, at ISI we appreciate loyalty. We want that out of our clients, so why should we be any different?

All of us at ISI also like the fact that the bank has supported us for a long time—ever since the late 1990s, when we were a struggling $1 million company and were barely turning a profit. I tell members of our staff to this day that "BancorpSouth believed in us before we believed in us." We appreciate that our BancorpSouth account team has been with us since 1998 and didn't just get on the victory train when the company grew into the $25 million business it is today. Through the years, BancorpSouth has also helped us navigate tough situations, like the embezzlement crisis in 2003, when we had that sticky situation of a whole bunch of forged checks. Later on, the bank also helped us to secure an important $3 million contract in 2009 with a significant increase in our line of credit—and they did this in the worst credit market in eighty years! That is the value of true partnering, which is why we appreciate the relationship so much.

Another key to ISI's partnering relationship with BancorpSouth is that ISI is 100 percent transparent in everything we do with the bank. We hide nothing from them. And in thinking through this, it's simple common sense. Look at the banking environment these days—talk about tough.

Since 2008, many banks have struggled just to survive. For example, the Troubled Asset Relief Program (TARP) was a program of the United States government, signed into law by President George W. Bush on October 3, 2008, to purchase assets and equity from financial institutions to strengthen the financial sector. A component of the government's measures in 2008 to address the subprime mortgage crisis, the TARP program originally authorized expenditures of $700 billion. And that was just to keep many of them in business.

Do you think any bank has had a huge tolerance for risk the past few years? Common sense told us at ISI that we needed to make sure the bank felt good about loaning us the money we needed to grow, and in doing so, we would provide whatever they needed, including additional documentation and assurances and guarantees related to the financial crisis of 2008. In return, the bank could be a part of a successful growth plan. Help them help ISI was our motto. Interestingly enough, do you want to know who is almost as excited about ISI's growth over the past few years as we are? You got it—our bank!

In 2011, our relationship grew even stronger when ISI was added to the bank's regional advisory board. It's been a good way to reinforce the relationship and get a keener understanding of the bank's business model.

So what does all this mean? In order to grow a business in difficult times, it is critical for small business owners to properly view their bank as not just a financial institution that charges them interest on loans, but as a valued partner who can help them grow. Establishing a trusted partnership can pay big dividends for many years to come!

Stepping Up to the Plate

Key points to help your business grow rather than plateau:

1. **Avoid complacency.** Businesses that get complacent will die, sooner or later. A business constantly has to adapt, evolve, and change to continue to grow, but standing still is not realistic in today's hypercompetitive marketplace.

2. **Prune the tree.** In order for a business to grow, it has to constantly reinvent itself. In many start-ups, the employees who help you build the business often don't have the DNA to adapt and change as it grows. As the business owner, you need to prune away the employees who will hold you back. It's a tough but necessary call, and if you delay your decision or fail to make it at all, your company will be putting all its energy into reviving dying branches instead of growing to new heights.

3. **Prepare for growth structurally and financially.** To prepare for future growth, a company must define its staffing requirements, establish tight controls on accounts receivable, and have access to adequate capital or a line of credit.

4. **Take it as a team.** Growing a business during a recession is tricky and risky, but don't take on all the pressure yourself. Educate your management team about all of the issues and challenges. Solicit their input on a regular basis. Make them

part of the solution. And keep your team and employees motivated with a clear vision of a successful future.

5. **Make your bankers your friends.** The dated strategy of a strained relationship between business owners and bankers no longer works. You need the bank's help to grow your business, so make them part of your team any way you can. Use their resources wisely and keep them constantly informed of what's going on with the business. In today's challenging economic environment, one thing bankers particularly hate is surprises. Communicate with complete transparency in all your dealings, and you'll find that your bank can be part of the success formula.

CHAPTER 8

NOT GROWING BROKE

A s we went through Doug's book, we knew what we needed to do in order to grow, in practical terms of staffing and structure. But as time went on, we discovered that this was only stage one of deciding to grow. In order to keep growing long term, we needed to enter stage two. We needed to take a psychological approach and focus on our mindset.

I read a book titled *Mindset: The New Psychology of Success* by Dr. Carol Dweck (Random House, 2006), a well-respected professor of psychology at Stanford University. In her book, Dweck talks about the extensive research she has done in identifying what she believes are the two basic mindsets that people have today: the fixed mindset and the growth mindset. I had to admit I was intrigued with this concept and what it meant to ISI and where I wanted to take the company in the future. Were some of my employees wired for growth while others just wanted to keep the status quo? Was this mentality simply embedded in their DNA? Was there any way to affect it? Before I could answer that important question, I had to understand the whole concept of mindset better.

To paraphrase Dweck, people with a fixed mindset believe their talents and abilities cannot be improved through any means. They feel that, one way or the other, they are born with a certain amount of talent and typically don't want to challenge their abilities, due to the possibility of failure. Even more problematic, they frequently guard themselves against situations in which they feel they need to prove their personal worth. And people with a fixed mindset frequently view challenges negatively, instead of as an opportunity for personal growth.

Conversely, people with a growth mindset believe their abilities, such as athleticism, business aptitude, and mathematical capacity, can, over time, be improved through hard work and persistence. In other words, work hard and you can get better at most anything. This sounded a lot like the successful people at ISI. Unlike people with a fixed mindset, those with a growth mindset tend to rise to the challenge when presented with an obstacle. Often, people with a growth mindset do not fear failure; instead, they view it as a chance not only to improve themselves but to achieve at levels they never thought possible.

Dweck explains that mindsets begin in childhood, extend into adulthood, and can drive multiple aspects of people's lives, ranging from parenting and relationships to sports and work. She reveals how prominent members of a variety of fields—business, literature, music, science, and sports—possess the growth mindset to achieve personal goals and dreams. One powerful insight I got from this book was that anyone can change their mindset at any age or at any stage in life—in fact, it lists specific steps and ideas to follow to achieve a growth mindset.

After thinking it through, I've realized that the real challenge for small, growing companies who have been around a few years is *mindset*. Even if you start out planning for growth and wanting to grow, as time goes on, some people develop a fixed mindset and find themselves stuck.

Business owners who develop fixed mindsets might regularly say things like, "That's the way we've always done it." They have a comfort zone that doesn't typically embrace new processes or strategies. But what are they really saying? As Dweck points out, at the end of the day, the mentality really is focused on a fear of failure. They are scared of what might go wrong.

Will that work in a growing business? Obviously not. As an entrepreneurial business owner, it is your job to communicate the value of changing. It's what we said earlier about how what got you here won't keep you here. Change is inevitable in any business, particularly in the technology industry, and if you don't embrace it, your business will die.

ISI is a vastly different company today than we were five, ten, and fifteen years ago. In the technology industry, that would be expected, right? We must constantly reinvent ourselves to not only survive but thrive. How does a business reinvent itself over time?

Growing from $260,000 in sales in 1996 to more than $25 million in 2011 is pretty impressive and took a lot of hard work to accomplish. I believe ISI's growth is a direct result of the number of people we have hired who have a growth mindset. We have hired people who constantly look forward to the company's future success and freely embrace the challenges related to new products.

An early example of this was back in 1998, when we did our first implementation of telemedicine in a local hospital. The telemedicine niche was just starting to develop, but all of us at ISI recognized that there was an opportunity to grow the company with this product. We had no clue what we were doing, but we felt like this was a market niche worth pursuing—as a result of a growth mindset.

Similarly, in early 2000, one of ISI's clients asked us about installing some audiovisual equipment in one of their conference rooms. It wasn't complex, but there were several projectors, podiums, and microphones we had never seen before.

Were we out of our comfort zone? You bet. Was it risky at some level? Absolutely. But it was a nice-sized contract we needed at the time, even if it wasn't in our wheelhouse. So what did we do? If we had had a fixed mindset, the likely answer would have been, "Sorry, but we don't do that kind of work. We're a video-conferencing business." And that would have been that.

But with our growth mindset, our answer was, "We're glad to help any way we can, and although we haven't done a lot of this kind of work, we will see that it is done right." ISI chose to rise to the occasion with persistence and hard work, and we got the job done to the customer's satisfaction. We saw this as an opportunity to improve the company and grow like we had never grown before.

And what do you think happened after that? From that first installation in 2000, ISI has grown the audiovisual portion of our business from $50,000 in revenue to more than $10 million in 2011, and it has been a key ingredient in the company's growth strategy. All because of our mindset. We wanted to grow and were willing to risk the chance of failure to embrace a new product line.

Now, with all the challenges in the current economy, is it realistic to have a growth strategy? And if you're like ISI, how much growth can you handle? What kind of growth do you want? If you start growing again, can you do it while protecting your values, reputation, and profitability? These are the key questions to answer in order to implement a successful growth strategy.

Also, look at your competitors over the last few years. What kind of reputation did they cultivate? Are there new competitors that have popped up? Was anybody growing like crazy before the recession? Are they still around?

During a recent discussion about growth at ISI, we talked a lot about how we felt the need to grow and how we wanted to go about doing it. We concluded that not growing the business when an opportunity presented itself was not an option. We have been playing a hot hand with our growth strategy so far, and we needed to continue to do so. Our clients, prospects, and industry were all telling us to do so.

With an aggressive company, you always want to keep moving and keep ahead of the curve. Most of us have heard the famous saying from hockey great Wayne Gretzky: "I skate to where the puck is going to be, not where it has been." That's ISI's mantra, and it has worked for us for a long time.

Also, as mentioned earlier, people at ISI are like most people in that they enjoy being a part of a growing company that offers opportunity of advancement and personal growth. We have a lot of people who have hung with us during the current recession and have worked diligently to maintain our reputation and keep us profitable. As the owner of ISI, I feel like we owe it to everyone, including our customers, to innovate and grow when it makes sense.

However, it is possible to grow too quickly. Finding the right growth rate requires self-examination of your business. You have to look at your business culture and values and see what kind of growth you can support. This is a big key to implementing a successful growth strategy, and it is not easy.

As I've said before, I am a conservative person by nature. Generally it has served us well, but when is it time to take a risk? Because I'm the owner of ISI, deciding how to handle ISI's growth rate is a personal decision. Certainly there is my own tolerance for risk, which is not very high. But even more than that, there are the resources required to support the growth.

Back in 2004, when we were on pace to double business from 2003, it was beyond exciting. We were booking business like we had never done before, and it was so gratifying. We had almost gone out of business the previous year because of a $250,000 employee embezzlement, and then we grew from $5 million in sales to $10 million in one year. Not bad, huh?

On the surface, it would all seem good with the big increase in sales, but the reality was that it was a grind for twelve long months. We did not have one of the basic ingredients for growth: the resources to support the increase in business.

We had an endless number of meetings about recruiting (and retaining) technical personnel to be able to keep up with the rapid pace of the work. And that's where we learned a valuable lesson in 2004. As business owners, it is imperative that you understand the dynamics of your business and have the discipline to live within your means and values, which may limit growth but ensure long-term survival and sustainability.

Can a small business owner ever have the guts to turn down business? As I think about the approach that has worked for ISI through the years and has really helped us through the current recession, it comes down to a concept that Jim Collins (author of *Good to Great*) describes in his new book, *Great by Choice* (HarperBusiness, 2011).

The concept of the Twenty-Mile March describes highly disciplined people and companies that gain success by understanding and sticking to the achievement of certain milestones despite the obstacles and discomfort that inevitably occur, along with the discipline to hold back from exceeding set limits even during good conditions. Many industry analysts and business school professors recommend never to take one single job larger than (at most) 20 percent of the total company revenue. Jim Collins calls it "fantastic discipline" when a company can set strict upper and lower limits to manage company resources and finances.

At ISI, we have implemented a very disciplined approach to revenue growth since 2004, when we really learned our lesson: Don't outrun your headlights. While doubling business was a lot of fun, it almost put us in financial jeopardy and caused considerable strain on employees, clients, and suppliers. That is why from 2005 to 2007, ISI grew at a very measured pace. Of course, that pace was somewhat dictated to us after the summer from hell.

When we really started growing again in 2008, we did so by using many of the strategies associated with the Twenty-Mile March and had the discipline to accomplish goals every day, month, and year. And we constantly reviewed these numbers to keep us on track.

Any variance in the plan was reviewed and adjusted. Looking back on it, that was the secret behind posting record sales in 2008 of $14.5 million—and doing so in a year that was the worst the US economy has seen in living memory. We grew to a level we could support technically and financially. And we maintained that same discipline to grow the business again in 2010 (after a dip in 2009), which helped us get to $17.5 million that year.

The lesson is to grow at a measured pace and have the resources and finances to support the growth. Interestingly enough, in 2011, ISI had an opportunity to dramatically grow the business with a $8.3 million contract in Arkansas.

We paused to consider it. Does this make sense? What happens if this deal goes south, and we are delayed getting our money? How do you finance $8 million in 2011?

If we had implemented the Twenty-Mile March strategy, ISI may have chosen to not pursue this opportunity, since it was a lot more than 20 percent of our forecasted revenue. In fact, that one contract represented almost 50 percent of our previous year's revenue in 2010. And that was a record sales year! So how does a business make a decision about such a lucrative opportunity?

In ISI's case, it came down to addressing a few issues: (1) Did we have a good track record for service and support of this account? The answer to that question was yes, and we had been doing well with the account since 2006. (2) Did the account have a good track record with us? Did they pay invoices in a timely manner? The answer was yes to both questions and they had been doing so since 2006. (3) Were there any requirements in the contract that we simply couldn't live with, or any unreasonable demands? The answer to both of these questions was no. The contractual requirements were as fair as they could be, as were the demands and requirements for ISI. (4) Would this contract harm ISI financially or otherwise? The answer was no, as long as we collected payment on invoices in a timely manner. (5) What was the downside if ISI didn't do the deal? That final question was perhaps the most important. We decided that there would be worse results if we didn't do the deal, like losing control of a key account, inviting our competitors in, and harming our reputation with other clients and suppliers. Simply put, the risk was greater to walk away than to actually do the deal.

And the best part of all this? ISI used a growth mindset in dealing with the big contract. We chose to set aside any fear of failure, get out of our comfort zone, and rise to the occasion. In the end, we did win the $8.3 million deal and posted record sales in 2011, growing again from $17.5 million to $25 million that year.

Stepping Up **to the Plate**

Key ways your company can practice disciplined growth:

1. **Hire employees who have a growth mindset** and continue to reinforce that mindset by the actions you take as a company.
2. **Understand the dynamics of your business and have the discipline to live within your means and values.** Candidly assess your tolerance for risk and don't try to be somebody you're not.
3. **Don't outrun your headlights** and take on more business than you have resources to support. Get an accurate sales forecast to get ahead of future needs.
4. **Set an upper and a lower limit on sales contracts, with the largest ones representing no more than 20 percent of total forecasted revenue** unless there are special considerations that deem it a necessity.

CHAPTER 9

SECOND CHANCES

I have always believed in giving people second chances. I guess I think that everybody is entitled to make mistakes. No one is perfect, right? Maybe I am just a sucker for a hard luck story. Or maybe it's just the way I am made. I got a second chance in my career. A big one.

After I was fired back in 1995, I got a chance to start a business. And seventeen years later, by the grace of God, it has grown into a $25 million company. Sometimes you just need to get a jump start to get your career going. And sometimes you just need someone to cut you some slack and give you a break. Either way I have carried that mentality throughout my career as CEO of ISI.

One of the perks of owning your own business is that you can choose not only who you want as employees but also how you want to manage them. Although ISI does have an employee handbook and professional human resources support, sometimes it simply gets down to a gut feeling in handling troubled employees.

There is also a practical side to turning employees around rather than just letting them go. Employee turnover is expensive! At ISI, we calculated that replacing even an entry-level installation tech can cost more than $60,000 in salary, benefits, training, travel, and more to get to an acceptable level of competency. And that's just the financial portion of the story.

The soft costs of turnover are the loss of productivity and disruption with suppliers, customers, and fellow employees. If you can retain an employee, it is almost always good for the business. Even more than that, how about the gratification derived from having a positive impact on someone's life? In my opinion, there is no way to put a price tag on that.

One example is an employee who joined us a few years ago after going through some really tough times. Prior to joining ISI, he was doing manual labor (like mowing yards) just to get by. His life had unraveled after his business shut down several years before. He just needed a break.

He was in the unemployment line and reaching the end of his rope when he contacted me. He said, "I read your book and know you have a lot of experience with hard times. Any chance you have something for me at ISI? I need a job. I'm not too old that I can't learn something new, and I know how to work. Can you give me a chance?"

It took me just a few minutes of thought and prayer before I called my VP of operations in. "Go find this guy something productive to do for us," I said. "He doesn't know anything about the technology, but he knows how to work." I added.

"Anything else I need to know?" he asks.

"Yes," I said. "This is not charity; this is business. This man deserves a second chance."

Later that day, I was thinking, *Why should I own a business and not be able to run it the way I want to run it?* These are just the kinds of things I feel good about doing. There's a sign prominently displayed over my desk that says LEAD WITH YOUR HEART. In my definition, lending a helping hand to a friend in need is leading with your heart, and it felt good.

So what's happened to this guy since we've brought him on board? It's remarkable, really. The first year was a little rocky, as he had to work through a pretty steep learning curve, but he kept plugging away. Then the light came on, and he started to show some serious progress. He began doing high-quality work and getting some good feedback from ISI operations management and fellow workers. And even better, ISI's biggest clients have been specifically asking for him to be on site to do their install work. A year after being on the unemployment line, he is now not only employed but doing good things at ISI, all because we gave him a second chance. Sometimes that's all that people need.

Yet another example happened about a year or so ago. It might not have been as dramatic as our guy in the unemployment line, but it was an important time nonetheless. We had a young man who had been working in our customer service department for years, handling an assortment of technical issues on a daily basis. It seemed like this guy could fix anything that was thrown at him. The more complex the better; that's where he shined. He was the MVP of our customer service help desk, year in and year out.

Maybe it was when the call volume went up and ISI started getting eighty to a hundred service tickets instead of forty or fifty. Or maybe we were running into problems that were even more complex than ever. Whatever the reason, our guy seemed to slip. He started missing appointments and not informing customers. Customers were not happy, and it was becoming a major problem. He was also not telling the truth about where he was spending his time when he was going from one job site to another. Great reasons to terminate a guy, right? Who wouldn't? This guy looks like a train wreck in every way imaginable.

In the previous chapter, I stated that sometimes you have to prune the tree in order to grow. And to do that, you need to look at your employee in terms of what he or she is contributing today, not just in the past. In cases like these, it's important to realize that when you look at an employee's performance today, you're really making a bet on tomorrow. The question in this case was whether this employee's performance today was indicative of his future performance, or was it worth an investment now for greater performance in the future? This is certainly an intuitive decision, and a matter of the heart.

We believed that we had to look at the history of this young man at ISI. Had he always had these kind of problems, or was he going through a bad time? If it was just a bad time, were there more bad times in the future, or could we safely say, "this too shall pass?" (And could we live with it until it did?) Or might he just be in the wrong department? As the owner of a business, you have to be able to make the tough call. There was certainly no clear-cut answer; you're damned if you do, and damned if you don't.

So what did I do? It was pretty simple, actually. I sat this young man down and explained to him that his behavior was not only unprofessional but unacceptable. Also, because I had also known him since he was a kid, I wanted him to know I took a personal interest in his career at ISI and needed him to get back on track, because it would break my heart to have to let him go. But let him go I would if he didn't get his act together, and get it together quickly.

And that's the important point: You can't give your employees second chances unless you get to know them on a deeper, more meaningful, and personal level. I took a special interest in this young man because I already knew a lot about him. I knew his mother and his father. I remembered when he earned his Eagle Scout award. I remembered when he went off to college. We had history in our relationship, and employees appreciate that.

After that first "come to Jesus" meeting, he and I sat down and really examined what was happening and what we could do about it. One thing we found out was that when the workload increased significantly, he simply couldn't multitask like he once could.

He also disclosed that he had been diagnosed with attention deficit disorder, which meant that many of his issues were health-related, not intentional nor malicious. Attention deficit disorder affects approximately 4 percent of adults, according to the National Institute of Mental Health. These adults have problems with organization, time management, sustaining their attention, completing tasks, and controlling their emotions.

So after we identified why we were having many of the problems with this employee, we had to decide what to do about it. We simply sat him down and assessed what he was good at and where he could be most productive, considering his health issues.

We broadened our search to other departments that needed his skill set. We identified a place where he could use his programming and technical skill and do things one at a time. He was able to escape the crazy multitasking world he struggled in and shift to one that was better suited to his talents.

Terminating him would have been the easy way out. It takes time and effort to retain an employee. But in the end, it can yield a lot of dividends. Today, that same employee is doing some of the best programming work we have done in years. It's like he's an entirely different person. And all it took was somebody believing in him.

It also goes back to a core philosophy I have for all of us at ISI. I want this company to represent a land of opportunity for our employees, and we want everyone who works here to be all they can be in their careers here. Most of our employees have started at one level and moved up into bigger and better jobs with more responsibility over time.

For instance, Derek Plummer, my VP of design and engineering, started out by himself as my primary engineer and installer back in 1997, and through the years he has built a department of some of the best designers and programmers in the country. Similarly, our CFO, Annelle Hochhauser, started with the company after the embezzlement crisis in 2003. Not only did Annelle have to deal with putting ISI's finances back in order, she also had to deal with a new software system and a state sales tax audit.

When she helped us get through all of those multiple messes, we gave her a special award signifying her role in slaying the three-headed monster. Annelle has been loyal to ISI for a long time and has grown her department from her Lone Ranger role in 2003 to five managers who handle accounts payable, accounts receivable, purchasing, expediting, warehouse, and executive support.

And there's our VP of sales, Jeremy Johnson. Jeremy started with ISI in late 2005 as a territory rep and was promoted to VP of sales in June 2010. Since then, Jeremy's sales team grew the business from $17.5 in 2010 to $25 million in 2011, and he is continuing his success today. How does this happen? Certainly the business growth has a lot to do with it, but I also think it has a lot to do with company culture. When a company has a culture that promotes innovation and creativity and also rewards initiative and success, that's a winning formula.

Stepping Up to the Plate

Key ways you can give your employees second chances in your business:

1. **Make sure you know why you want to keep this employee.** Keep it professional, but recognize the personal side of business as well.

2. **Assess the advantages and disadvantages to your company.** Do not keep an employee because you feel sorry for him or her. Do what's best for the business (and ultimately for your employees as well).

3. **Don't engage in special treatment.** Do not set up special rules for these employees because of past problems. Treat all employees equally and in a fair and professional manner.

4. **Listen to your heart and look into theirs.** There is no perfect formula for employee retention decisions. It's an inexact science at best. Listen to your heart and look into theirs, and let that be your guide to whether it is worth your while to retain a troubled employee.

CHAPTER 10

MOTIVATING THE MILLENNIALS

One of the key ingredients to ISI's success in growing and sustaining business in the current recession has been what makes many businesses strong: our people. But in ISI's case, it's not just the people, it's our *young* people. Most of ISI's employees are under thirty years old and barely out of college with minimum work experience, if any. Most of them are barely older than my own children, and truth be known I feel almost that close to them. By virtue of hiring them I've protected them from what 10 percent of the local community has been dealing with for several years: the unemployment line. I feel responsible not only to employ them but also to coach them and make them productive. It's a winning formula for both parties.

As I mentioned earlier, the sales team farm system approach was put together by design to bring on new energetic people who could be trained the ISI way. Through the last few years, that strategy has extended to other departments as well, such as technical support, design, and engineering. ISI is loaded with young, energetic people who are driven to succeed and have done so in some very difficult times. But how did that happen? How do you get high-level performance out of the Millennial generation? Some people may wonder if this is even possible from the "participation trophy" generation. (Remember the movie *Meet the Fockers*, when Robert DeNiro walks into his future in-laws' house and, looking at a wall of awards and trophies, remarks, "I didn't know they made ninth-place ribbons!")

Young people in this age group are commonly referred to as Millennials. For the first time in history, four different generations find themselves in the workplace. In addition to the Millennials, born between 1981 and 2000, there is Generation X, born between 1965 and 1980; Baby Boomers, born between 1946 and 1964; and the Greatest Generation, born before 1946. I am a fifty-six-year-old Baby Boomer and the parent of two Millennials, and I grew up as the son of parents who were part of the Greatest Generation. Like most of you, I can personally vouch for the fact that each generation has its own history, expectations, and values, which often clash with those of different generations. With such different DNA, how does a Baby Boomer (like me) motivate a Millennial? For me, it starts with attempting to understand them. So let's take a quick look at the history of each generation and the values and expectations each brings to the workplace.

No matter what generation you're in, most people would agree that the Greatest Generation was aptly named. This was the generation that came of age during the Great Depression and World War II and went on to build modern America. This generation was united not only by a common purpose, but also by common values: duty, honor, economy, courage, service, love of family and country, and, above all, responsibility for oneself.

Only the members of the Greatest Generation, like my parents, could tell us what the Great Depression was really like, because they were there. Both my father and mother lived through it, and like everyone at the time, it changed them forever. It began in 1929 and only really came to a close when unemployment had fallen from its high of 24.9 percent in 1933 to 4.7 percent in 1942. In fact, I can remember my father telling me that at the ripe old age of 12, he had to use his paper route money to support the family after his father lost his job at the railroad. Industrial production had fallen by as much as 46 percent. The stock market had lost as much as 90 percent of its value and left many people penniless. Bank failures were rampant, and even the most conservative American citizens lost their savings overnight because there was no insurance for depositors. In 1940, unemployment was still hovering around 15 percent, with no relief in sight.

Kids as young as fifteen were looking for a way to help out and voluntarily risked their lives to be soldiers instead of going to school—for one reason. They did it so they could put food on the table for their siblings and parents. The end of this horrific episode of American unemployment really didn't change until 1942. And truth be known, the end of the Great Depression was not the result of monetary or fiscal policy, but rather the December 7, 1941, surprise bombing of Pearl Harbor and Adolf Hitler's subsequent declaration of war on the United States.

This ignited a massive nationwide build-up in the US armed forces, ultimately putting over 15 million men in uniform and another 50 million men, women, and children to work supporting the war effort. Everyone pitched in to do their part with half of the United States' 133 million people working in support of the war. It was a historic effort on many levels at home and abroad that helped turn the tide for the Allies. On May 2, 1945, World War II was officially over and the Greatest Generation was victorious. From that point onward, their world changed, and an age of plentiful jobs and unimagined prosperity was upon them.

Interestingly enough, many thought the end of World War II would increase unemployment rolls, with all the soldiers coming back home and looking for work, but the demand for goods and services actually created millions of new jobs. Demand was increased in many other ways too: There was pent-up demand from sixteen years of hard times in the Depression and rationed goods through World War II. Technological advances made during the war paved the way for incredible demand for things like low-cost televisions, washing machines, and refrigerators. Soldiers returning home were also looking for low-cost housing which drove construction. And there was another phenomenon that developed after World War II, starting in 1946. Babies were being born at a record pace, creating a whole new market for goods and services. Thus the Baby Boomer generation became the largest population niche in the history of the world.

The pieces were certainly in place for the Greatest Generation to achieve what everyone wanted after all the difficult years they had endured: to truly live the American Dream. But how did they achieve the dream? Two words: *hard work.* Not being highly educated, that was all that most of the Greatest Generation had to work with. In fact, only 30 percent of Americans graduated from high school in 1930. As noted earlier, many of them had to forego their education to do whatever work they could to help support their families.

Contrast this with today's numbers: over 70 percent of Americans have graduated from high school and 27 percent of those have a bachelor's degree or higher. When you stop and think about it, it's unbelievable that the Greatest Generation achieved the greatest jump in the American standard of living with just a good work ethic and the desire to own a refrigerator and a television. But they weren't just materialistic; they wanted to improve the world for their children so they would never have to experience what it was like to be hungry or cold, or experience the many hardships that characterized their own childhood.[13]

Now let's look at the children of the Greatest Generation. How have the Baby Boomers tried to make their mark on the world and pass that along to their children, Generation X and the Millennials?

Baby Boomers were born after World War II, between 1946 and 1964, and are now predominately in their fifties and sixties. Through the years, many Baby Boomers have worked hard to be well established in their careers and hold positions of power and authority. The children of the Greatest Generation were taught valuable lessons about the value of hard work and professional achievement and working your way "up the ladder." Why are Baby Boomers like their parents in some ways, and in many ways so different? And why is their way so different from their children's way, the way of the Millennials (and, to some extent, Generation X)?

Let's start with their attitude about work. Baby Boomers are all about work. Many of us are defined by it. It is who we are. Many of us are extremely hardworking and motivated by position, perks, prestige, and all that goes along with that. Frankly, we all have wanted more than what our parents had, as each generation tries to improve on the previous one. Isn't that what we've always heard? Baby Boomers seem to relish long work weeks and define themselves by their professional accomplishments and recognition. Since many of us sacrificed a great deal years ago to get where we are in our careers, my workaholic

---

13   Kathleen Brush, "The Next Greatest Generation, Please Stand Up. The Economy Needs You," Examiner.com, September 9, 2010, http://www.examiner.com/article/the-next-greatest-generation-please-stand-up-the-economy-needs-you.

generation believes that Generation X and Millennials should pay their dues like we did. In essence, they should conform to the culture we believe is the right one and the only one we have known—overwork yourself and let everyone know it!

Many Baby Boomers today are quick to criticize the younger generations for their lack of work ethic and total commitment to the workplace. When it comes to work ethic, many Baby Boomers like me have a lot in common with the Greatest Generation and possess a strong drive to succeed. I know myself that part of what drives me every day is that I think of how hard my father had to work at twelve years old to help support his family and put food on the table during the Great Depression. I often think that my worries of today are child's play compared to what he had to deal with in the 1930s.

Also, much like the Greatest Generation, Baby Boomers believe in hierarchal structure and rankism and have a hard time adjusting to workplace flexibility trends. We tend to believe in traditional work environments, highly value "face time" at the office, and fault younger generations for having the desire to work remotely. Of course, we've also been known as the Woodstock Generation, and many Baby Boomers welcome exciting, challenging projects and strive to make a difference and change the world.[14]

The Millennials, in contrast, have been labeled the most demanding and most coddled generation in history.[15] (Although, who's really to blame for that?) Unlike their grandparents, they don't have a world war to influence their experience of the Great Recession or (for Americans) inspire unabashed patriotism or confidence in their country. Instead, they are stressed out about their future, much more so than their parents and grandparents. Statistics show that 600

---

14   Sally Kane, "Baby Boomers," About.com, accessed March 21, 2013, http://legalcareers. about.com/od/practicetips/a/Babyboomers.htm.

15   Ron Alsop, *The Trophy Kids Grow Up* (Jossey-Bass, 2008).

percent are more stressed about their future than young people were in 1938.[16]

But the biggest difference between Baby Boomers and Millennials, in my opinion? Millennials truly want to live life on their terms and not conform to someone else's standard, which is a vast difference from the Baby Boomer mentality. In fact, from what I've observed, they dislike it greatly when anyone tries to characterize their generation in generalized terms.

So how do you manage them? What's a winning strategy? I can start by saying what won't work: the old 1970s style of motivation. Baby Boomers know what I'm talking about. Remember those days? How did management get their point across? With lots of screaming and yelling and threats. "Myers, if you don't make your quota next month, you're fired!" Do you know how many times I heard that? And the funny thing was, I was a guy who was *making* his numbers. I pitied the guys in my office who weren't doing as well. Their jobs were a living hell. But that was the way it was done in those days: management by intimidation and all results-driven. No trophies for ninth place in those days!

At ISI, I've had a few clashes with my young workers through the years. One such episode was over a simple thing like the dress code in the office on casual Friday. This individual not only wanted to wear jeans to work but also have his shirt out like he was going to a backyard barbecue. After a short coaching session, I informed this individual that his definition of professional and my definition of professional were totally different, and don't dress like that again. We clashed and disagreed, but I didn't yell or threaten him (like my old bosses would have done)—and we both moved on.

---

16   Kathleen Brush, "The Next Greatest Generation, Please Stand Up. The Economy Needs You," Examiner.com, September 9, 2010, http://www.examiner.com/article/the-next-greatest-generation-please-stand-up-the-economy-needs-you.

I've found that a successful approach to managing the younger generation (or any generation) all starts with one word: *respect.* In order to motivate any employee, young and old alike, you have to start with respect. You have to respect them first as people and second as your employees; that is critical. However, I also have to constantly remind my young workers that they're not entitled to my respect (or anyone else's); they have to *earn* it by doing things like overcoming adversity, working hard, and being competent in their job.

Respecting your young workers as people means that you understand them and are interested in what they want out of their job and their career goals and aspirations. It is also important to understand that the Millennials are not Baby Boomers 2.0. They do not want the same things out of a career that employees did in the 1960s and 1970s. Why is that? Think about it.

The Millennial generation has seen events in their brief time on this earth that no other generation has seen in recorded history. Events like September 11, 2001, when almost 3,000 people lost their lives at the World Trade Center and the Pentagon, representing the worst terrorist attacks in US history, all seen on live TV with images shown over and over again for more than a decade now.

And if that wasn't enough to rock their world and create enough of a sense of uneasiness, then how about the economic meltdown of 2008? Many of these young people experienced firsthand what it felt like when their parents and grandparents got laid off from their jobs. Uneasiness and uncertainty? You bet. And how about the look on their parents' and grandparents' faces when they realize their lifelong savings have shrunk 50, 60, and 70 percent, and they are forced out of retirement and have to go back to work?

All of these events have shaped the Millennials' thinking. And like it or not, that thinking is very different than that of most Baby Boomers. Millennials tend to see jobs as a means to an end. It's not that jobs and work aren't important, but, unlike Baby Boomers, they refuse to let work define them.

Millennials also tend to have a different set of work-life values than Baby Boomers. While Baby Boomers tend to be work-obsessed, Millennials are demanding flexible schedules that allow them to pursue an active life away from the office. We've definitely had clashes about this at ISI: Many times I have to remind my young workers that I don't like clock watchers, and if that's the way they want to work, they are probably not in the right place. The funny thing is that even my young workers that go home right after five p.m. will typically be on their smart phones or computers until late at night working on projects, returning emails, and so on. They're just not doing it at the ISI office, which is old school to them.

In light of all of this, and in addition to the basic value of showing respect, ISI has a number of strategies that create a productive and profitable work environment that still honors the values and strengths of young people. First, ISI actively promotes a culture of collaboration

Bonding with the Sales Team. *Enjoying a night at the ballpark with Josh Wilbanks (left) and John Milford (right).*

and teamwork that appeals to our young people. The environment at ISI encourages teamwork and creativity on a daily basis.

Millennials also prefer clear direction—as opposed to Baby Boomers like me, who tend to like autonomy. We've had to face this issue head-on when it comes to accountability, which, frankly, has been one of ISI's struggles. A few years ago, I had just completed a performance review for a young salesman who had a fallen short of his quota from the previous year. In fact, this was the second year in a row that he had done that, so I felt it important to sit him down and spend extra time explaining how important it was to make his numbers so that the company could run efficiently and continue to grow in the future. Afterward, I was confident that I had made my point crystal clear, and he totally understood what was going on and knew exactly what was expected of him.

Know what happened next? He got his paycheck a few weeks later and asked me, "Are we not doing raises this year?" I was dumbfounded. My first thought was, *Is he deaf? Did he not hear what I said about making his numbers?* So I sat him down again and explained Accountability 101, which in sales means that if you don't make your numbers, you don't get a raise—pure and simple. I further explained that ISI didn't dream up the quota numbers and that these were the sales totals we needed to run the business. I also challenged him by letting him know ISI would no longer support a mediocre performance.

After thinking through it a little more, I realized that part of the problem with this employee was not just with him but with ISI. We simply didn't do a very good job of setting clear expectations of the goals for this employee or securing the commitment to achieve them. We also needed to do a better job of managing those expectations throughout the year as well as providing feedback, good or bad. And last, our employee needed to more clearly understand the consequences when he didn't make his quota (for him and the company). We needed to constantly evaluate this employee's effectiveness—all year long.

Now what do you think happened next? This same salesman got the message and not only made his quota two straight years but also grew his department sales more than 50 percent in 2012. What was the secret? The simple matter of holding him accountable.

Accountability simply means making sure everyone is pulling their own weight and making positive contributions to the organization, and it is crucial for Millennials who prefer more direction. In fact, it is a pretty simple strategy, and maybe using the acronym SIMPLE is the best way to explain it. S stands for "set expectations," I stands for "invite commitment," M stands for "measure progress," P stands for "provide feedback," L stands for "link to consequences," and E stands for "evaluate effectiveness."[17]

At ISI we constantly reinforce that high performance and success are not dependent on one simple factor, nor are they the result of one or two things. It's not one big sale or one good month that makes ISI successful, but rather the daily, weekly, and monthly effort that has built the business over the long haul and holds everyone accountable for their work all year long.

Another motivator for Millennials at ISI is leveraging some of the latest technology to do their jobs more effectively. Millennials love technology, so giving them a chance to work with the latest in smart phones, mobile video conferencing units, and high-definition audiovisual technology plays to their strengths in that area and is a great way to attract bright young talent. On the other hand, conflict sometimes arises, since my young workers all want to have the latest technology equipment and I can't afford to buy it all. Most of my young people love the latest gadgets, but we have agreed that it

---

17   Brian Cole Miller, *Keeping Employees Accountable for Results* (AMACOM, 2006), 2–3.

has to be a product we can make money on or we can't afford to buy it. They don't like that answer sometimes, but most seem to understand it.

We are also big on work-life balance at ISI, which includes providing flexible schedules to accommodate personal needs such as school schedules or other family matters. Many of our young employees also have the option to work from home using our video conferencing technology to maintain contact with management. I admit I'm more of a traditional office guy and have gotten irritated with several employees who wanted to telecommute and work from home. I have documented cases where ISI got burned letting people do this, when it was really an excuse to take the day off. But through the years, ISI has selectively used our video technology to allow several of our young people the ability to work from home to take care of sick children or spouses and similar situations. I'm happy to report we have people productively working remotely in several locations.

Another ISI strategy that has worked well for us has been the ability to maintain an environment where everyone's voice is continually heard, young or old. If you have a good idea for a product or service at ISI, we want to hear about it, and we invite everyone to offer input. Our young people in particular love the fact that they have their personal stamp on several ISI health care and network solutions. And last, ISI doesn't put a ceiling on our young people's paychecks. Depending on their position with the company, many of them have the ability to earn above-market wages and have fun as well. However, I do insist that they earn what they get. I have told them many times that although I don't limit their income, I also don't pay "show up" bonuses. Whatever money they get, they need to earn it—plain and simple.

So, is there any real magic formula to motivating the Millennials? Not really, but the following strategies have worked for us at ISI.

Stepping Up to the Plate

Key ways to motivate Millennials:

1. **Recognize that the old style won't work anymore.** It's not the 1970s anymore (that's a good thing!), and you must adapt your style to your audience. Don't try to manage by intimidation.

2. **Show respect.** The Millennials have witnessed 9/11, the Great Recession, and other gut-wrenching world events. Life has not been perfect for them, either. Hear that, Baby Boomers?

3. **Meet them halfway.** Millennials aren't defined by work, so don't expect them to be. Allow them to achieve work-life balance with concepts like remote offices and flexible schedules.

4. **Promote a creative culture.** Young people want their voices to be heard, so listen to them. Several ISI products and services were developed by our young employees.

5. **Don't limit the earnings potential of young employees.** Depending on the job, use their energy and drive to your company's advantage.

AIMING HIGH

've always been a big fan of setting goals, whether it be for myself or for ISI. How can anyone ever achieve anything worthwhile unless they have something to shoot for? A business without goals is like a ship without a rudder, and that never seemed right to me. And for ISI, I have always tried to set the bar as high as I can and have all of us reach for the stars.

As an example, in the early days of the company, we set a goal to win the *Memphis Business Journal* Small Business of the Year Award. After we were nominated, ISI went through a rigorous series of on-site interviews with a panel of judges who evaluated various aspects of the company, such as financials, community involvement, office facilities, and employee engagement. The process itself was highly competitive with a number of other companies vying for the award, but in the end ISI came out on top. Everyone in the company took time to celebrate, and we were all proud of the accomplishment, but we didn't stop there.

After earning the Memphis Business Journal award in 2001, ISI was also recognized as one of the fastest-growing companies in the state of Tennessee, and then later as one of the fastest-growing firms in the southeastern United States. Time to stop? Not ISI. We wanted more! So we decided to expand our reach not just to the Southeast but across the entire country, which is why we threw our name in the hat for the Inc. 500 award back in 2001.

Inc. magazine was founded in Boston by Bernie Goldhirsh, and its first issue appeared in April 1979. Goldhirsh was an MIT-trained engineer who worked at Polaroid and on ballistic missiles before becoming an entrepreneur and founding *Sail* magazine, which he sold for $10 million, using the profits to start *Inc.* Like many entrepreneurial ventures, *Inc.* was founded to fill a void in the marketplace and serve as a resource for entrepreneurs and small business owners.

The Inc. 500 is an annual list of the 500 fastest-growing private companies in the United States, which was introduced in 1982. Some of the more notable companies that have made the Inc. 500 list include Microsoft, Oracle, Timberland, and Under Armour. The Inc. 5000 is an expansion of the Inc. 500, which ranks the country's top 5000 fastest-growing private companies and also features a special ranking of the top 10 percent of the list as the Inc. 500.

Did we really think that ISI could be named one of the fastest-growing private companies in the United States? Talk about a lofty goal! But that's how a business has to think in order to achieve. And at ISI, I have always preached two words: *Think big!*

In 2001, there was nothing bigger for us than making the Inc. 500 list later that year. The Inc. 500 list is widely acknowledged as the best of the best in small business and is a worthy goal for any entrepreneur.

I'll never forget the feeling that all of us had when we got the official notification letter informing us that we had made the Inc. list at number 182. It would have been nice to have been number one, but making the top 200 in the country wasn't too shabby either.

ISI had arrived! We were now being recognized as one of the top private companies in the country, and the feeling was exhilarating for everyone in the company.

A short time later we even staged a reception for ISI employees, customers, suppliers, and friends in recognition of the Inc. 500 award. It was a great time to thank everyone who had helped ISI achieve such a significant award. And it was also a motivator. *This was so much fun; let's do it again,* I was thinking.

Breathtaking Success. *ISI VP of sales Jeremy Johnson celebrating another year of making the Inc. 5000 list.*

And why not? How about making the Inc. 500 list again? How crazy would that be? But that's exactly what we did two years later in 2003. Not many companies make the Inc. 500 list twice, and we were all very proud of the accomplishment. But there was more to it than just receiving another award. As a company we got used to winning.

We got used to achieving; it was in our DNA. We wouldn't accept mediocrity at any level. We had a reputation to uphold, and we knew it. And we kept growing and made the Inc. list again in 2007, and again in 2009, 2010, 2011, and 2012—seven times in total since 2001 we had made the list of fastest-growing private companies in the United States and earned placement on the Inc. Honor Roll for making the list five or more times.

Rarefied Air. *ISI makes the Inc. 500 list of fastest-growing private companies in the United States for the seventh time since 2001. Celebrating at the 2012 conference are Jordan Myers (left), Michael Sanders (center left), Norm Brodsky of Inc. magazine (center right), and Brad Kirby (right).*

And how many Inc. 5000 companies have done that? Fewer than 5 percent, we were told. Perhaps making the list in 2012 was the most gratifying of all. ISI had grown 96 percent from 2009 to 2011 in three of the toughest years the US economy has seen in living memory and joined CDW, Publix Super Markets, Levi Strauss & Co., and Facebook on the 2012 list.

We were part of a very exclusive club, and it felt really good. And maybe it was even more satisfying because the path to get there had not been easy. We kept working hard and made a conscious decision to not let the recession be an excuse for losing sight of our goals. We kept our eyes on the prize.

But we never quit. And with creativity, resilience, and tenacity we hit the all curveballs that had come our way and ultimately used crisis to not only strengthen but also grow our company like never before.

Growing a business in any economy is tough, but in a recession, it seemed almost impossible at times. So many things were working against us, yet we managed to not only survive but thrive in the toughest business environment in eighty years. Make no mistake about it: None of it has come easy to us, and we had to hit a lot of curveballs to get to where we are today. But I can assure you from personal experience that the strategies outlined in this book not only have worked for me and my company, but they can do the same for you and your company as well. Let me know how you're doing by emailing me at jmyers@isitn. com. Also check out the company website at www.isitn.com. I wish each and every one of you the very best in your business and your life!

ACKNOWLEDGMENTS

Special thanks again to my wife, Maureen; son, Jordan; and daughter, Katie, who have provided me their love, encouragement, motivation, and unwavering support throughout my career. Nothing that I have accomplished in my professional life could have been done without the three of you, and for that I will always be grateful. In writing this book, many of the difficult challenges we faced as a family came back as vividly as if they happened yesterday. Your courageous response to those challenges, then and now, is a constant source of inspiration to me.

To my late parents, Dorothy and Jerry Myers, and my late brothers, John and Charlie Myers. I think of and pray for each of you every day and work hard to honor our family's name in everything I do at ISI and in the community.

To all dedicated ISI employees: It is a testimony to your hard work, tenacity, and creativity that the company has continued to grow and thrive through some of the toughest years our nation's economy has seen in living memory.

To all ISI clients, partners, and suppliers: Thanks for continuing to believe in us and helping us grow the company in the most challenging of times. Your ongoing support and friendships mean a lot to all of us.

To all my family and friends who have been so supportive of ISI through the years: Thank you for continuing to always be in our corner. We couldn't have made it through the last few years without you.

Thanks to David Hancock, Margo Toulouse, Bethany Marshall, and everyone at Morgan James for your help and support in making this book possible. Thanks also to my gifted editor, Amanda Rooker, whose expertise, professionalism, and encouragement have helped me so much in getting this book written. It really means a lot.

To Julie Kremer and all my friends, legends, and fellow campers at the New York Yankees Fantasy Camp for their friendship and support.

To the University of Memphis basketball team for the opportunity to speak to the team and a day I'll never forget. Go Tigers!

To Mimi Uhlmann and all the folks at Memphis Catholic High School who are a part of the Education that Works program. ISI is proud to do our part to help out a great program.

To, Eric Vic, and everyone associated with the Seed Hatchery program for doing what you do to help entrepreneurs in the Memphis area to pursue the American dream.

Thanks to Duke Walker for all the help in getting the photos for this book ready for publication. You did an amazing job!

And finally, thanks to everyone at St. Patrick's Church, and God bless you for supporting the neediest of the needy in Memphis and truly doing God's work on a daily basis. ISI is proud to do what we can to help you with your mission.

ABOUT THE AUTHOR

Jay B. Myers is the founder and CEO of Interactive Solutions, Inc. (ISI), a Memphis-based firm that specializes in video conferencing, distance learning, telemedicine, and audiovisual sales and support.

Myers started ISI in 1996 and in the past sixteen years has built it into a $25 million company with sixty-one employees and offices in Memphis, Nashville, Chattanooga, and Knoxville, Tennessee, as well as Birmingham, Alabama; Oxford, Mississippi; and Little Rock, Arkansas.

ISI has received numerous corporate awards and recognition in the past several years, including being named to *Inc.* magazine's list of the fastest-growing private companies in the United States seven times in the past eleven years, and was recently featured in the Small Business section of the *Wall Street Journal.*

ISI was also named the *Memphis Business Journal* Small Business of the Year in 2001, and in 2003 it was the first recipient of the Kemmons Wilson (founder of Holiday Inn) Emerging Business Award.

Prior to starting ISI, Myers earned numerous sales awards while working for international corporations such as Eastman Kodak and Hewlett-Packard.

In 2007, Myers published his first book, *Keep Swinging: An Entrepreneur's Story of Overcoming Adversity and Achieving Small Business Success*, and was awarded the 2010 Ethan Award for success as an entrepreneurial author.

Myers is active in numerous local community organizations and currently serves on the board of the Chickasaw Council (Boy Scouts of America) and BancorpSouth (advisory board). He has also recently been named chairman of the board of the Better Business Bureau of the Mid South. In 2011, Myers was inducted into the Christian Brothers High School Hall of Fame.

Myers lives in Collierville, Tennessee, with his wife Maureen and their black lab Casey, and has two children, Jordan and Kaitlin.

Special Dedication. *Chuck (right) with my daughter, Katie.*

On January 23, 2013, we lost an important member of my family when our fourteen-year-old black Labrador, Chuck, passed away. As you can see by the picture, he was loaded with personality and always wanted to be in the middle of everything, no matter what we were doing. Chuck was everything you wanted in a family pet: handsome, loyal, and fun. I will miss him greeting me every day on the way to and from work. RIP Superpup. We will see you again on the Rainbow Bridge.